AF559862

AUTOMATED LIBRARIES

AUTOMATED LIBRARIES

By

Dr. Bipin A. Patel

M.A., & M.lib., Ph.D.

Librarian

Himatnagar Nagaric Shahakari Bank Ltd.

Science College, Himatnagar (Gujarat)

(India)

DISCOVERY PUBLISHING HOUSE PVT. LTD.

NEW DELHI-110 002

Published by:
Namit Wasan

DISCOVERY PUBLISHING HOUSE PVT. LTD.
4383/4B, Ansari Road, Darya Ganj
New Delhi-110 002 (India)
Phone : +91-11-23279245; 23253475; 43596065
E-mail : discoverybooksindia@gmail.com
discoverypublishinghouse@gmail.com
namitwasan9@gmail.com
web : www.discoverypublishinggroup.com

***Reprinted:* 2020**

***First Edition:* 2014**

ISBN: 978-93-5056-407-3

Automated Libraries

Printed at:
Infinity Imaging Systems
Delhi

Preface

Major traditional libraries particularly the academic libraries turned to electronic or digital libraries and offered information services without boundaries. The library users could access library resources from any where at any time. The changing face of the library services supported the life-long learning environment and toward developing the learning society in the country. The automated library systems to the library has made these things happened. This book addresses the acquisition and deployment of technology affecting such development. The contents of this book deal mainly with the automated libraries materials. The remarks are of a general nature and concern the basics of library materials acquisition. They are based on the author's professional experience. Each library has to adjust the details of its acquisition procedures to its own environment.

—Author

Contents

1

Library Automation: An Introduction

Library automation is the application of ICTs to library operations and services. The functions that may be automated are any or all of the following: acquisition, cataloging, public access (OPAC and WebPAC), indexing and abstracting, circulation, serials management, and reference.

Automating a school library is the process which restructures its functions and reinvents its services. By keeping a database as the basis, automation converge new technologies of information storage and retrieval with traditional housekeeping operations. An automated school library can serve the teaching and learning community more effectively. A reduction in the time needed for routine operations can be utilized to give customized services to the users. The process of library automation has a short history in our country. It needs proper planning and active implementation. Kendriya Vidyalaya Pattom initiated the automation of its library to cope with the ever changing needs of the students and staff. The modernization of the Library Media Centre helps the students to become skilled information users and life long learners.

DEFINING LIBRARY AUTOMATION

Library automation may be defined as the application of computers to perform traditional library house keeping activities such as acquisition, circulation, cataloguing, reference and serials control.

Automation is used to reduce the amount of staff time devoted to repetitive (and often less challenging) activities that must be done in any properly functioning library. It is to remember that, various library operations are automated, not the library as such.

HISTORY OF LIBRARY AUTOMATION

Punched cards were invented by Hollerith in 1880 and used in tabulating the US census data. The library at the University of Texas was perhaps the first to use punched cards in 1936 for circulation control. The Library of congress used the unit record machines for the production of catalogues in 1950. Many libraries in the US followed the system for automating their activities.

Library automation entered into its second era in 1960s with the advent of computers. The notable ventures were MEDLARS, MARC, etc. Until the early 1990s, "automating the library" involved generally the same features as those in place since the advent of machine readable cataloguing record in the late 1960s.Libraries created integrated text based systems using micro/mini computers in which traditional library housekeeping operations were computerized using the library's database as the foundation.

In the last decade, library automation has undergone a transformation that reflects changing definitions of library service in general and access to resources in particular. The introduction of global networking such as internet, cheap availability of technology and new media technologies made information more accessible.

Today's integrated library systems must not only provide modules which automate traditional library functions but also capable of connecting through the local systems into systems of other information or knowledge suppliers, databases and internet.

INSTITUTIONAL LIBRARY AUTOMATION

Institutional libraries started automation in the West in 1960's. Many schools in the US and European countries automated their library operations in a large scale in 1980s with the advent of microcomputers. Nowadays they are integrated with modern information networks which allow the students to access up-to-date information with ease.

INDIAN SCENARIO

In1962 INSDOC experimented the preparation of a Union Catalogue of scientific serials. The Documentation Research and Training Centre (DRTC) introduced *Docfinder* (a computer used for finding documents) in 1968. The library automation in India was a slow process and got momentum in 1980s. Research and technical institutions were the forerunners and academic libraries followed them. New professional library management software packages entered in to the Indian market and some Indian companies also tried to make it with Indian flavour.

Some libraries run by Public Schools became automated in late 1980s. More schools entered in the foray in 1990s with more funds and infrastructure. The schools in Govt. sector those had good libraries had been following the conventional library concepts and never looked for automation due to lack of funds.

New millennium witnessed tremendous developments in Information and Communication Technologies (ICT), and the concepts of school libraries changed from mere storehouses of books to well-organized library media centers with variety of services (online and offline). Some educational institutions were the torchbearers, but most of them are lagging miles behind

THE CATALOGING MODULE

- Used for the creation, storage, retrieval and management of bibliographic records and/or indexes.
- Usually there are two different interfaces for search and retrieval of the electronic catalog : one used by the catalogers that allows them to maintain the library database (the main cataloging module), and one provided for users that allows them to search

and display the results – the Online Public Access Catalog (OPAC).

- A third interface for search and retrieval of the catalog which may or may not be present in some systems is the WebPAC

A PRACTICAL APPROACH TO LIBRARY AUTOMATION

INTRODUCTION

Library automation refers to use of computers, associated peripheral media such as magnetic tapes, disks, optical media, etc., and utilisation of computer based products and services in the performance of all type of library functions and operations. Computers are capable of introducing a great degree of automation in operations, functions since they are electronic, programmable and are capable to control over the processes being performed. The utilisation of computer and related techniques make the provision to provide the right information to right reader at the right time in a right form in a right personal way. Automation of library activities provides the services very efficiently, rapidly, effectively, adequately and economically.

The modem libraries and information a center facilitates free communication because access to information has become a fundamental right of the clientele. The automation is economically feasible and technologically required in modem libraries to cope up with the requirements of new knowledge, the enormous increase in the collection of materials, problems of their acquisition, storage, processing, dissemination and transmission of information. The capabilities of computer associated peripheral media and its application in library activities and services led to a highly significant quantitative and qualitative improvement especially in online technology. Information/ knowledge itself is of no value. It is the use of information that makes it valuable. This is our and users key to a more success, more happiness in ours mission. put this information to work for user by automation of library functions. The role of computers and their associated peripheral media are being increasingly used in library and information services for acquisition, storage, manipulating, processing and repackaging, dissemination, transmission, an improving the quality of products and services of library and information centers.

FACTORS FOR LIBRARY AUTOMATION

GROWING INFORMATION AND SHRINKING SPACE

The enormous growth or information explosion of literature in each area, subject in number and size and results fragmentation of literature and increasing specialisation in every field of knowledge. Due to this information explosion, the quantity, variety and complexity of information are being increased rapidly in every field. Computer application can solve this problem, as it is capable of storing huge bulk of information on tiny storage mediums, *i.e.*, a CD-ROM can store the text of the complete set of Encyclopaedia Britannica. Serials, abstracts, indexing periodicals, etc., are already available on CD-ROM.

INCENSEMENT OF USERS AND ORGANISING THE FLOOD OF INFORMATION

Increasing the number of clientele of library and information centers and their specialised desires forces us to change the method of organising information because traditional methods is going to become inadequate. The manual method has serious limitations and, facing problem to provide access to reader's information that is available in a wide of publications from so many sources.

COST HIKE OF PRINTED AS WELL AS ELECTRONIC READING MATERIALS AND RESOURCE SHARING

The rapidly enhancement price of information materials motivated the library and information centers to share their resources. They realise that the only way they could fulfil their client groups is by effective cooperation between libraries, information centers and networks and by sharing of all type of resources.

ENHANCEMENT IN BUDGET

As increasing the members of the library, cost of information materials, services and growth of information or information explosion, the budget of the libraries is also raised. That is also allowed us to automate the library activities and make maximum utilisation of the library funds.

AREAS AND SERVICES OF LIBRARY AUTOMATION

Library automation is generic term used to denote the various activities related with the location, acquisition, storage, update, manipulation, processing, repackaging or reproducing, dissemination or transmission or communication, an improving the quality of products and services of library and information centers. It enhance the speed, productivity, adequacy and efficiency of the library professional staff and save the manpower to avoid some routine, repetitive and clerical tasks such as filing, sorting, typing, duplication checking, etc., on which we can conserve costly professional manpower for technical service' and readers service. The main activities and services of library automation are given below.

INFORMATION RESOURCE BUILDING

Acquisition of books, monographs, audio-visual, electronic materials such as CD-ROM, maps and so on. There are some specific functions of an acquisition process. Suggestion, recommendations and selection of library collection:

- Duplication checking, library holding checking.
- An vender selection.
- Preparation of order, cancellations of order lists with terms and conditions of the supply. Checking of overdue orders.
- Record of items on order.
- Record of received and non-received items and receipt to the vender.
- Items verification with order file and invoice.
- Inspection of items by the concerned department.
- Prepare for payment after accessioning.
- Prepare budget and maintain accounts and statistics subject wise, etc.

- Final report. Items, subjects wise, chronologically, booksellers report, etc.

DATA ENTRY

Database is required for each

- Books
- Clients/ members
- Serials
- Audio-visual
- CD-ROMS, Floppies
- Gifted items
- Maps, Reports, etc.

CLASSIFICATION AND CATALOGUING

- Catalogue card production.
- On-line cataloguing.
- Duplication checking of catalogue cards.
- Production of duplicate catalogue cards.
- Preparation of authority file subject heading list.
- Shorting, checking and filing of catalogue cards.
- Automatic generation of added entries (author, title, series, etc.). Generation of monthly accession list.
- Developing centralised and on-line cataloguing.

CIRCULATION CONTROL

- Registration/ cancellation and make bound time for membership.
- Issue, return, renews reservation of documents and produce the slip for proof.
- Charges for late, lost book, binding and production of penalty slip.
- Maintenance of circulation. Statistics.
- Inter library loan.
- Use of bar code system.
- Report statistics of circulation.

SERIAL CONTROL

- Input essential serials data.
- Order list of new serials.

- Mode of payment, prepare for payment.
- Receipt and updating the records.
- Receipt to vendors or publishers.
- Preparing the list of present holding, additions, missing, cancelled serials chronologically, subject-wise, etc.
- Renewal and cancellation of present subscriptions.
- Sending reminders and follow-up of missing issues.
- Binding control.
- Accession register of bound serials.
- Prepare budget and maintain accounts statistics such as subject wise, binding, etc.

DOCUMENTATION AND ALLIED SERVICES

- Indexing and abstracting of micro and macro documents. Thesaurus construction.
- Compilation of union catalogue.
- Bibliographic control.
- Current awareness services.
- Literature search.
- Selective dissemination of information.
- News paper clippings.

INFORMATION RETRIEVAL

- Database creation and maintenance, interactive searching, saving of in house as well as external databases.
- Search and print outs of quires against specified requirement.
- Such as about the books (issued, reserved, lost, overdue, weed-out), membersship, inter library loan, penalty charges, periodicals, newspaper clippings, reports, etc.
- According alphabetically, chronologically, subject-wise, members-wise, keywords with each particular such as accession no-wise, title, author, call number, edition, etc.

LIBRARY COOPERATION

Cooperative acquisition, cataloguing, and coordinated information services, Resource sharing.

Access to Database:

- Information service
- Back up service
- Document delivery

CD-ROM Services:

- Information searching
- Text delivery

Online search:

- Access to Database
- Downloading

E-mail:

- Electronic mailbox Bulletin Boards

Access to Internet:

- Information superhighway
- Cyberspace
- World Wide Web (WWW)
- DIALOG and other databases.

TRAINING OF THE LIBRARY SOFTWARE

- Self demonstration programme.
- Help menu and software manual.
- Separate training model for library professional and as well as for users.

SELECTION OF SOFTWARE

To offer the complete satisfaction of users and perform the library activities and functions, we must select a competent and suitable software which can meet out our requirements or can be developed on contracted basis by any software company or can be developed by professional of the institution keeping in view the requirements of the library. An increasing numbers of library software companies and their attractive advertisements/ propaganda's confused the libraries which software is very much meet with their needs. Libraries and information centers must keep in mind some basic aspects before selection of library software.

A library automation committee is to be constituted which includes library and computer software/ hardware experts. Prepare a list of your library's areas, activities, services and functions which are to be automated.. A profile of the library software's is to be made. Consult with the same organisation/ libraries about software and their functions, which are already, automated their services. The experiences of the other librarian who have used software are more valuable than the assurances of the manufactures. Let the vendors demonstrate their product. Library and computer software experts should prepare a observation report of library and software facts, which meet or how much meet or do not meet our requirements and submit it to the chairman library automation committee.

Consider the services after installation, but de not believes on unjustifiable assurance, made by companies' representatives and make agreement of all fact. Consider the market reputation of manufacturing company, software or vendor. Software selection is a very complicated issue, on the observation of experts, the discussion should be made by the selection committee and most suitable in regard of flexibility, capacity, expandability, security, economically, user's friendly, module based and updated with the latest technology is to be procured. There are some leading names of the software packages which are available in the market may be competent with your needs.

LEADING SOFTWARES

- *LIBSYS:* Most widely used in India, fully integrated multi-user system design to run on super, micro, mini, computer under UNIX/ VMS/ LAN platforms. Micro libsys, a subset of libsys is also available for PC's under DOS/ XENIX. It can be modified to operate on any preferred database such ORACLE, INGRES, etc.
- *SCIMATE:* Introduced by Institute for Scientific Information is designed for use with IBM- PC, "the Apply -II, the TRS- 80 model- II micro-computer running on the micro processors Z -80 or 8086 supported by CP/ M -80 operating systems.

- *CDS/ISIS:* (Computerised Documentation Service/ Integrated Set of Information System), developed by UNESCO, distributed in India by NISSA T free of cost is table driven, generalised information system focused for handling non-numerical information of any volume, with special features of advanced programming in PASCAL. It has a version that runs on disk operating system VST, MVS or DOSIVS or IBM 370, 303x. 43xx., its mini-micro version can be run on PDP- II series or on IBM- PC (XT -AT) or compatible microcomputers.
- *MINISIS:* It is very powerful, comprehensive and easy-to-use software developed by International Development Research Centre (IDRC), Canada to run on HP 3000 family of computers. MINIS IS is compatible to renowned ISIS software which run on IBM 360/370 main frames and conforms to the ISO 2709 and UNIMARC international formats for interchange of library data. HP 3000/37 is the low-end member of the powerful, interactive family of HP 3000 computer system which are ideally suited for information management and transaction proceeding. This system along with the MINSIS software provides very attractive and cost effective solution for the needs of small to medium sized libraries in India.
- *SANJAY:* Automated CD/ISIS package for library: With the development of CDS/ISIS capabilities by DESIDOC is being implemented as a model in Technology Bhawan, Library.
- *MAITRAYEE:* This software package is an attempt to bring library computerisation and networking aspects on and integrated platforms, commissioned by CMC LTD., a Government of India Enterprises, NISSAT, die the complete feasibility study and come out with the well defined functional specification.
- *OASIS:* This package has three modules standard, advanced and special, can be operated on any

compatible micro computer using MS and PC DOS-3.1 or higher equipped with 640 of RAM and IBM recommended 80 MB hard disk.

CONFIGURATION FOR COMPUTER HARDWARE

Generally the configuration of computer hardware is depend upon the size of the library which include the total collection of items such as strength of books, journals, clienteles, services, functions and type of the library. Normally more than one Lakhs holding we consider it a large size library, medium sized library having more than 50,000 holding and less than this, its called small library.

Table 1.1 Difference between Large, Medium, and Small Sized Library

Large-sized Library	Medium-size Library	Small-sized Library
Pentuim-3 Computer with	Pentuim-3 Computer with	Pentuim-3 Computer with
64 MB RAM	32 MB RAM	16-32 MB RAM
3-4 GB Hard Disk Drive	1.2 GB Hard Disk Drive	1 GB Hard Disk Drive
150 MB Cartridge Tape Drive	150 MB Cartridge Tape Drive	150 MB Cartridge Tape Drive
5.25, 3.5" Floppy Disk Drive	5.25, 3.5" Floppy Disk Drive	5.25, 3.5" Floppy Disk Drive
UPS/CVT	UPS/CVT	UPS/CVT
VGA Colour Monitor	VGA Colour Monitor	VGA Colour Monitor
8 Port Intelligent input! Output card	8 Port Intelligent input! Output card	8 Port Intelligent input! Output card
X.25 Card with Driver Software For Networking	X.25 Card with Driver Software For Networking	X.25 Card with Driver Software For Networking
Terminal 5-7	Terminal 3-5	Terminal 2
Laser printer, Ink-jet and Dot Matrix Printers	Ink-jet and Dot Matrix Printers	Ink-jet and Dot Matrix Printers
MODEM (56 kbps Modem for communication).	MODEM (56 kbps Modem for communication).	MODEM (56 kbps Modem for communication).
CD-ROM Drives	CD-ROM Drives	CD-ROM Drives
TCP/IP	TCP/IP	TCP/IP
O.P.- DOS, MS-DOS, WINDOW, UNIX or XENIX etc	DOS, MS-DOS, WINDOW, UNIX Or XENIX etc	DOS, MS-DOS, WINDOW, UNIX Or XENIX etc
Bar-code system with software	Bar-code system with software	Bar-code system with software
Lamination machine	Lamination machine	Lamination machine
Telephone lines 2	Telephone lines 1-2	Telephone lines 1

TRAINING AND ASSISTANCE FOR LIBRARY AUTOMATION

The training of the library staff in computer operation is of vital importance. Every library staff member should be given a general orientation about the computer system. Training should begin much before the computer system is installed because the whole process depends on the library staff. Mostly the supplier of the hardware and software provide training on two levels, general aspects of system operation, and training on specific areas of operation at a higher level, which is free of cost. This training is very much practical because the staff will work with the machine and if there be any trouble, it can be rectified.

The training should be in house training and in the actual work situations and these training programme and planning must be a part of the vendor proposal in the final agreement There may be external experts in hardware and software application to make the training more knowledge-based job-oriented. Training facilities for library automation are available in various parts of the country at a low cost supported by NISSAT. There are many organisation and professional bodies! associations which are conducting basic computer training as well as library oriented training program's. They also guide them of software selection, hardware selection, and installation of software and operations of day to day library functions. Other than the NISSA T there are many organisations which can provide the help and assistance in library automation. These are INSDOC, DESIOOC, DELNET, BONET, CALIBNET, PUNET, DRTC-Banglore, INFLIBNET Ahmadabad, etc.

LIBRARY AUTOMATION IN INDIA

GROWTH OF COMPUTERS IN THE COUNTRY

Computerisation had its beginnings in India when punch cards were used during the late 1950s and early 1960s. Computerisation activities can be said to have started in India in 1955 with the installation of the first computer system HEC-2M at the Indian Statistical Institute (ISI), Calcutta. A second computer Ural, also installed at IS1 in 1958 followed this. In 1960s computers arrived in India. Mini computers started penetrating the market in late 1970s while microcomputers were introduced in the 1980s in the country. However, due to the high cost of mainframe and mini computers, use of punch cards continued till 1980s.

The shift from punch cards took place only after the advent of microcomputers, which were generally cheaper than the mainframes, and the minis and many institutions could buy them. The period between 1955-65 can be called as introductory phase during which 16 computers were introduced in the country. The second phase of 1965-72 can be termed as consolidation phase, 170 computers were installed in India by 1972. IBM had a lion's share (60-75 per cent) of the computers installed in the country in these phases. About 120 third and fourth generation systems were imported in to the country during 1976-81. IS1 and Jadavpur University jointly designed and developed the first indigenous computer ISIJU that was installed at Jadavpur University in July 1964.

However, the commercial production of indigenous computers started only in 1973 when the Electronic Corporation of India Ltd (ECIL) started manufacturing during 1973-78, it installed 94 computers in the country. The Indian computer industry has grown at a rate of about 10 per cent per year during late 1970s. Until 1985, India's contribution to computers and telecommunication technologies was practically nil. The main reasons are the non-receptive government policies and hostility from trade unions. This is why the computer revolution of the 1970s which marched ahead with full steam not only in the West but also in neighbouring countries like Singapore, Taiwan, Hong Kong, South Korea, Thailand and Malaysia, did not have a foot hold in India.

With the government formed in 1984 adopting technology-friendly policies, the situation started improving slowly. In 1966 the Hindustan Computers Ltd (HCL), launched a price war in microcomputers and the computer market in the country started growing. Many new companies rushed to encash the trend. By 1988 there were 250 manufacturers in the field. The total number of computer systems increased from 120 in 1970 to around 448 in 1978 and to 600 in 1980; this rose to 2000 computers in 1984 which saw a five fold rise to reach 10,000 in 1985 and about 1 lakh by the end of the Seventh Plan. There was a steady growth in the computer industry in the late 1980s.

In 1984 India had an installed base of 9,100 computers out of which 4,050 were manufactured in the country. By 1986, this number rose to 52,150 and 22,150, respectively. Fierce competition brought down the microcomputer prices. Still only elite institutions could buy them. Liberalised economic policy of the government and application of information technology saw the all round growth of the computers industry during the Eighth Plan. During this period the computer industry got impetus from the new computer policy announced by the Department of Electronics (DOE), Government of India in November 1994. The number of low cost PC-based networks and LANs increased.

There were an estimated 1,00,000 e-mail users in the country in 1995 which was expected to be doubled by the end of Eighth Plan. Production of computers using Intel's Pentium processor stabilised and many key sectors like Banking, Railways, Airlines, Oil, Power, Defence, Coal, S&T, Steel, and Education have started to induct computers during this period. The Indian computer industry has grown at a rate of about 10 per cent per year during late 1970s. In 1985 the production of computers had reached ₹ 2000 million. The Ninth Plan document of DOE expects to achieve a production value of ₹ 178.5 billion by the year 2001-02, with a cumulative growth of 46 per cent per annum. In the recent years, the production of PCs has registered a phenomenal growth.

The 286s, 386s and the 486s were taken out of production line. During 1996-97 a total of 4,67,387 PCs were produced of which more than 50 per cent (2,77,396) were Pentiums. In 1999, the country had an installed base of about 3.2 million PCs of which about 56 per cent (1.8 million) are 386 and above. This base is expected to reach 4.47 million in 2000 and 9.64 million by the year 2002. It has been estimated that about 50 per cent of home PCs sold are machines priced below ₹ 40,000. In 1998, about 1,65,000 PCs were sold with expected sales of 3,14,000 PCs in 1999 and about 5,00,000 in the year 2000. In the late 1990s, the computer industry (both hardware and software) has attained maturity.

This is the result of the new computer policy of 1994, the IT-friendly measures of the government including the IT Action Plan, and the realisation of the necessity of automation in all walks of life. During the year 1994-95 the growth was 60 per cent over the previous year. In recent past, the small and medium enterprises and the home market gained momentum and the falling prices helped boost sales. Although the growth in 1997-98 was only 20 per cent due to the slow economic growth and instability, it picked up in the subsequent year and registered a growth of 32.4 per cent. Although these statistics are encouraging, the PC density (number of PC's per 100 population) in the country is too low to be happy. This figure indicates the usage of PCs in various activities such as business, marketing, information retrieval, electronic messaging, e-mail, file transfer, and shows the extent of the penetration of computer culture in the society.

As per the International Telecommunications Union (ITU), in 1995 India had only 0.1 computers per 100 people or one computer for every 1000 population. This rose to 0.2 in 1998 and is expected to reach 2 by the year 2008. The developed countries have 10 PCs and above with USA and Switzerland leading with PC densities of 29.7 and 28.8, respectively. However, the falling prices of the PCs because of fierce competition between firms to have a niche in the market resulted in reduced value of sales. Unlike the initial brands the prices of latter brands like PC 486 and Pentium fell steeply. In just two years (1994-96) the prices of Pentiums fell steeply from about ₹ 2,00,000 to 45,000 finally settling around ₹ 30,000, the average selling value of a PC in 1999. Currently a Pentium 4 with 1.5 GHz clock speed desktop sells at around ₹ 45,000. All these resulted in increased computer literacy and made the computerisation a reality in all sectors in India.

DEVELOPMENT OF LIBRARY AUTOMATION SOFTWARE IN INDIA

While the software industry is a well organised sector, library software is largely confined to some premier institutions and their libraries. It is only recently that private sector entered this field. Even then, the aggressive marketing efforts as in the case of computer software are not there. Many of the library automation efforts using in-house expertise were around the existing PCs and software packages including dBase, and FoxPro. In some cases, high level programming languages like COBOL, BASIC, C, C++ and Pascal were used. Initially, only simple and important functions such as acquisitions, circulation and cataloguing only were automated; integrated packages were thought at a later date.

These efforts generally led to the development of a total integrated system (as in ISAC and DESIDOC), or were used to convince the authorities to purchase a library automation software from the market. In some cases, the vendor of the library automation software helped to convert the automated data into a compatible form for use with the new software. Firms like LibSys undertook creation of bibliographic records of the library holdings. Both the MARC and CCF formats are used now to develop bibliographic databases. After the introduction of CDSIISIS software package of Unesco in Indian libraries in the mid-1980s, NISSAT organised a number of training programmes on application of CDSIISIS to library activities in 1990s.

These courses, besides training the professionals in using the software, have made them aware of the benefits of library automation and also introduced computer culture among the LIS professionals. This also gave impetus to many institutions for developing their own library software suitable for their libraries with special emphasis on the routines and services important to the institution. Thus began the indigenous efforts towards developing integrated library software packages in the country. Some of the special libraries such as those at Bharat Heavy Electricals Ltd (R&D), Steel Authority of India Ltd (SAIL), International Crops Research Institute for the Semi-Arid Tropics (ICRISAT), INSDOC, NIC, DESIDOC, and IIT, Kanpur have successfully developed software for library automation. Specific mention is to be made of DESIDOC, which has developed three software packages. The first was named the Defence Library Management System (DELMS) and was developed in COBOL under multi-user Unix environment. This software was provided to the DELNET, and later to INFLIBNET under the name ILMS, Integrated Library Management System.

While DELNET switched over to Libris and DELSIS subsequently, INFLIBNET has developed a new soft package SOUL, Software for University Libraries. DESIDOC also developed a software package for NISSAT called Sanjay, an integrated library management software using Unesco's CDSIISIS in Pascal language. Later DESIDOC developed *Suchika,* an integrated software package in C++ language. The first version was developed in DOS and Unix platforms to suit small and large libraries. Later, *Suchika* version 2 was also developed on Windows NT platform. The Computer Maintenance Corporation Ltd (CMC), a public sector company specialised in computers, developed an integrated software package called *Maitrayee* suitable in library network environment.

The software was developed with NISSAT support for CALIBNET. INSDOC initially developed CATMAN to support cataloguing in the National Science Library. Recently, it developed *Granthalaya,* an integrated library automation software package. These institutional efforts inspired the software developing firms in private sector with the result that now many commercial software packages have been developed and marketed.

ACTIVITIES IN INDIA

Although some institutions like ISI and IITs in the country have imported mainframe computers in the late 1950s and early 1960s, priority was being accorded for productivity-and R&D-linked jobs. This is because of the huge costs involved in getting mainframes and also due to the fact that library work was generally viewed as not so important by the concerned authorities who accorded lower priorities in allotting computer time for such work. Many of the libraries and information centres started using computers for their work after the introduction of mini computers during late 1970s. Even these were generally costly, only elite institutions in the public, academic, R&D and private sectors could afford them and so, the libraries in these institutions were able to utilise them to some extent.

Library automation, as a result, did not progress satisfactorily. However, the arrival of micro-computers and personal computers (PCs) in the Indian market in the 1980s gave the necessary impetus; the environment began to change and library automation picked up momentum. The Indian National Scientific Documentation Centre (INSDOC), one of the pioneer institutions in library automation field, started using computers for information processing in 1964 utilising the IBM 1620 at IIT, Kanpur for its union catalogue. It also utilised the IBM 1620 at Delhi University for other related jobs. The Documentation Research and Training Centre (DRTC), Bangalore also started the computerisation work in the late 1960s.

A Document Finding System was designed and developed with programmes to prepare catalogues on tape which was later tested on the IBM 1401 system at ISI, Calcutta. In 1970, the library of NAL, Bangalore made efforts in computerising the circulation control with an ICL 1004 system. As per a survey conducted by Kamath, there were nine libraries which were using computers in the country. The various library routines where computerised procedures used by these libraries include:

- Procurement (one library),
- Charging and discharging of documents (one library),
- Cataloguing (two libraries),
- Preparing union catalogue (one library), and
- Preparing addition lists (four libraries).

INSDOC started providing computerized SDI service from January 1976 using the IBM 3701155 computer at IIT, Madras and the CANISDI software with CA Condensates database. INSPEC A&B databases were also used from 1977 for providing SDI services. In 1977 BHEL (R&D), Hyderabad started providing SDI services to the various units using computers.

During 1970s a few more libraries started using computers for library routines. Notable among them include the Tata Institute of Fundamental Research (TIFR), Mumbai and the

Space Applications Centre (SAC), Ahmedabad. A number of seminars and workshops were conducted on various facets of library automation during this period by national institutions like SIET, DRTC, BARC, and INSDOC.

This situation improved in the 1980s and the early 1990s with the launching of national and metropolitan networks. Further, during this period the prices of the computer hardware and software have started climbing down making them affordable to many libraries. Metropolitan networks like CALIBNET and DELNET, professional associations like ILA, AGLIS and IASLIC, and national institutions like INSDOC, DRTC, and SIET started training programmes in automation of libraries, bibliographic database development using CDSIISIS and other software packages. National institutions like DRTC, INSDOC and DESIDOC, were actively engaged in such programmes. INFLIBNET of UGC started providing financial assistance to the academic libraries for library automation.

Agencies like NISSAT also supported such activities. The INFLIBNET has, supported 123 universities/deemed universities towards creating infrastructure facilities including buying PCs and modems, developing databases, and getting telephone and Internet connectivity. It is also providing recurring grants for some activities for 5 years after the initial grant is utilised.

INFLIBNET expects to extend financial support for another 30 universities in the coming couple of years. These efforts paid rich dividends and resulted in a significant level of automation of academic and research libraries in the 1990s. The main players in library automation in the past decade have been the special libraries of the country. Most of these library and information centres are in the R&D institutions under the central government and in universities. These include the:

- Council of Scientific and Industrial Research (CSIR),
- Department of Atomic Energy (DAE),
- Defence Research and Development Organisation (DRDO),
- Department of Science and Technology (DST),
- Indian Council of Agricultural Research (ICAR),

- Indian Council of Medical Research (ICMR),
- Indian Space Research Organisation (ISRO),
- Public Sector Undertakings (PSUs) and the institutions of national importance like IITs, Indian Institute of Science (IISc),
- All India Institute of Medical Sciences (AIIMS), and
- National Medical Library.

Although special libraries took the lead initially, many university libraries and libraries from major institutions in arts, humanities, social and behavioural sciences, and management are increasingly participating in library automation. Some special factors favoured special libraries, which were able to undertake library automation. These include:

- Easier decision making due to the relative autonomy they possess being in publicly-funded organisations,
- The pressure these libraries experience to provide efficient services and better, wider access to information (this pressure is the result of the goals or deadlines to be achieved by the institution),
- The wide availability of PCs, and
- The free availability of Unesco's Micro CDSIISIS which facilitated easy development of databases.

Another factor is that in many of the institutions, internal talent was available in the form of computer specialists (programmers) who were responsible for the in-house development of library software.

LIBRARY SOFTWARE PACKAGES AVAILABLE IN INDIA

The library application software, integrating all the activities and routines of the library is an essential software for the libraries. There are many integrated library management packages available in the market suiting to the needs as well as budgets. They range from ₹ 10,000 to ₹ 6,50,000. Many are also available in multi-user network versions. Many authors have attempted comparative study, evaluation and selection criteria for Indian software packages. Researchers reported 19 software packages used for the automation of library activities in 1994.

Alice for Windows

Soft Link's Alice (Windows version) is a fully integrated library management solution. The DOS version is known by OASIS. Alice for Windows is the complete library automation toolkit, which incorporates the latest information technology, and functional depth, provides a complete range of library functions using discrete modules, and allows select modules that suit the individual library need. It has wide usage and currently being used by more that 8,700 libraries all over the world. In this dynamic world of information, it follows constant features upgrade enabling to meet all kind of requirements of all range of libraries.

Modules are grouped into Standard modules, Advance modules and Special modules. Standard Modules are required for a library to function from day to day. These are: Management, Reports and Utilities, Circulation and Enquiry (OPAC). Advance Modules extend the usability of the automated library. These are: Acquisitions, Periodicals, Communications, Guidelines, Journal Indexing and Remote Enquiry.

Special Modules are available for those libraries which have a specialised need. These are: Advanced Bookings, Book Review, Cooperative Cataloguing, Multimedia, Multi Lingual, Patron Self Checking, Rapid Retrospective, Remote Cataloguing, Resource Rental, Technical Manual, User Access Menu, User Definable MARC, Web Enquiry, Books Hire, CD-ROM Loader, Fines, Library Service, Interlibrary Loans, Professional Enquiry, Records Management, Report Generator, Self Circulation, Union Catalogue, User Definable Databases, Book Wizard Cont, Mobile Circulation

Features:

- It has four versions: Academic Library. Special Library, Public Library, and School Library versions.
- It runs on Standalone PCs irrespective of the platform including Windows, Novell, Linux, with an Apple Mac version.
- It supports 239.50 clients/server architecture, GUI, lntranet enquiry and system functions; Internet

enquiry functions for operating systems including UNIX.

- Export and import of data in MARC formats and data conversion from CDSIISIS, dBase, FoxBase, and from any other standard library software.
- It is multilingual and can work with such languages as English, Russian, Japanese, Chinese, Arabic, Spanish, French, Malaysian, Vietnamese, Thai, Hindi and other Indian languages.
- The software is being continuously upgraded; one or two upgrades are being released every year.

CDSIISIS

CDSIISIS stands for Computerised Documentation Services/Integrated Set of Information Systems. CDSIISIS is an advanced non-numerical information storage and retrieval software developed by Unesco since 1985 to satisfy the need expressed by many institutions, especially in developing countries, to be able to streamline their information processing activities by using modern (and relatively inexpensive) technologies. The software was originally based on the Mainframe version of CDSIISIS started in the late '60s, thus taking advantage of several years of experience acquired in database management software development. CDSIISIS is a menu-driven generalised Information Storage and Retrieval system designed specifically for the computerised management of structured non-numerical databases. One of the major advantages offered by the generalised design of the system is that CDSIISIS is able to manipulate an unlimited number of databases each of which may consist of completely different data elements.

Although some features of CDSIISIS require some knowledge of and experience with computerised information systems, once an application has been designed the system may be used by persons having had little or no prior computer experience. For advanced users having access to computer professionals, CDSIISIS offers an integrated programming facility allowing the development of specialised applications and/or the functional extension of the software as originally provided. It has the largest installed base of about 1390 installations and is a PC version available on a number of platforms like Windows 95, Windows NT, DOS, Claris, etc. It has a number of fields, records, alternate scripts, multimedia capability, and Web interface. Many specialised application products have been developed around CDSIISIS.

Besides in libraries, the package can be equally used to create databases. An ideal software package for small and medium-size libraries, it was distributed free of charge initially; now it is priced at ₹ 15,001. The package performs a variety of operations related to information storage and retrieval with powerful search capabilities and flexible database management.

It allows interlinking records from more than one database, use of more than one data sheet, and conforms to 180-2709. The major functions provided by CDSIISIS allow you to:

- Define databases containing the required data elements
- Enter new records into a given database
- Modify, correct or delete existing records
- Automatically build and maintain fast access files for each database in order to maximize retrieval speed
- Retrieve records by their contents, through a sophisticated search language
- Display the records or portions thereof according to your requirements
- Sort the records in any sequence desired
- Print partial or full catalogues and/or indexes
- Develop specialised applications using the CDSIISIS integrated programming facility.

Database Menu

The bottom part of the menu normally contains the list of the most recently opened databases. You may open any one of them by simply clicking on the corresponding entry. It also allows you to import data from external files recorded according to the ISO-2709 standard format for information interchange and also to extract a database or a portion thereof normally for transmitting it to other users. You may also use this command to perform some reformatting of the records of a database and then use the import function to store the reformatted data into the original or a different database. It also allows you to print the output of a given query and/or to print a selected range of records.

Browse Menu

It allows the whole database to be browsed or edited independently from any search performed; displays the list of searches performed so far, from which you may select the one desired. It also facilitates in displaying the record (according to the currently selected format) or displaying either the current format or the current record in ASCII.

Search Menu

It provides Expert Search and Guided Search—for a simplified search interface, and saving the search results. Saved searches can be recalled. Edit Menu: This facilitates data entry, deleting a record, copying records in ASCII or rich text format. Configure Menu: This allows you to change the language in which menus, windows, prompts and system messages will be displayed. When you select this, a list of available languages is displayed from which you may select the one desired. Once selected, a language remains in effect until you change it again. It allows display of the current parameter settings.

Utilities Menu

This allows you to add or delete a field with a specified contents to a range of Master file records. It also allows to add or delete or replace a field with a specified contents to all the records retrieved by a given search. Windows Menu: It arranges windows so that they overlap, starting in the upper-left corner of the main CDSIISIS window. Help Menu provides helps In troubleshooting while working with the software.

Windows Version (WINISIS)

The Windows version (compatible with Windows 3.1x, 95, 98, Me, NT4 and Win 2000), version 1.4 was released in January 2001 has been totally re-written in C++ language (as against Pascal in DOS and Unix versions). This move provides a common standardised language for all platforms - DOS, Windows, Unix, etc. This reduces maintenance costs, increases portability, and renders implementation of client-server architecture easy.

No conversion is needed when moving from CDSIISIS DOS to CDSIISIS for Windows. Same database and inverted files of DOS can be used here. Some changes in formatting language and displays however occur. It includes all the features of the MS-DOS version except some database utilities such as the database reinitialisation. It is designed for current MS-DOS users who wish to migrate to the Windows environment, as well as for new users.

DELMARC and DELPLUS

DELPLUS (formerly DELSIS), an integrated modular package, was developed on Basis plus by DELNET to support complex cataloguing and union catalogue functions under network environment. The software provides interface to CDSIISIS and supports creation of bibliographic records in 13 Indian languages (using GIST card). It facilitates duplicate checking, online help and interlibrary loan. Currently it supports all the DELNET databases catering to all the network users.

The software is ISO-2709 compatible. While DELMARC is designed for bigger libraries that have collections of more than one lakh, DELPLUS is designed for all types of small libraries with a collection of up to one lakh.

DELMARC Ver.1.0.0

This software is offered to Member-Libraries of DELNET with a collection of books up to 1,00,000 at a subsidised price of ₹ 15,000.

Special Features

- Software is compatible with bar code technology.

- It is designed and developed exclusively to work in all kinds of libraries including public libraries, academic libraries and special libraries.
- Multi-user facility allows different branch libraries/ sections/nodes of a library to function together.
- Free up gradation available.
- Follows internationally recommended standards and formats such as US-MARC, MARC21, UNIMARC, and UK-MARC.
- Provision for backlog entry, backup and restore facility and bar coded stock verification facility.
- Provides lists of country and language codes and also online help.

DELMARC manages libraries with extensive collections, complex operations and serves a large clientele. This software has been designed after a comprehensive study of different library-related functions performed in different kinds of libraries. This software is easy to work with and offers the Acquisition, Cataloguing, Circulation, OPAC, Administration, Export/lmport, Authority Control Article lndexing Report Generation modules. The module for Serials Control is being tested and will be released soon.

Acquisition

The acquisition module enables library staff to handle the following major function related to acquisition of library material: Suggestions management, Approvals, Ordering, Cancellation and Reminders, Receiving of Documents, Accessioning, Management of Vendors, Publishers and Currency Tables.

Cataloguing

Cataloguing of any type of material in any MARC format using AACR II rules, Category of material like reference special, etc., can be defined, The shelf No. Can also be given to the item that will be useful in stocktaking, Cataloguing of Multiple Copies, Copy of a record, Backlog Entry facility (Retro-Conversion facility).

Circulation

Takes care of all possible functions such as issue, return, reissue, reservation, etc. Member enquires and maintenance of the status of materials can be handled. Complex functions like fine management for each category of users and material can also be effectively carried out. Issue, return or reserve items by Accession No. as well as by Title, Author, etc., and Overdue charges.

OPAC

Individual search (by Author, Title, ISBN, Accession No., Subject, Class No., etc.), Boolean search, special search (for cataloguing purposes), are possible. Provides the new arrivals' list, online reservation of new arrivals or other titles.

Administration

Researcher define the Member Categories, Member Groups, Currencies and their exchange rates, Acquisition Modes, Payment Modes, Material Categories, Miscellaneous Services, Select/ Unselect MARC tags, holidays, user passwords, etc., that will be used throughout the functioning of the software. Administrator can delete data or restore the deleted data like Members' Records, Vendors' Records, Catalogue Records, etc., Generation of Report., Allotment of privileges to members, SDI facility, Other operations like Receipt Block Generation, setting the members' Photo File Format,

Export/Import

Export/import of data intolfrom any standard MARC format. Authority Control enables to maintain Author, Title, Series and Subject Authorities and links with the records. Article Indexing maintains a database of various articles indexed in the library or collected from outside sources. Member/Vendors' Maintenance can add, edit or delete the member'slvendor's data. Member's photo is automatically picked up from the directory once scanned. Reports: A wide range of reports are generated including Vendors' List,

Ordered Materials, Received Material, Overdue Orders, Missing Items, Written-Off Items, Reserved Items, Issued Items, Members' List, Stock Verification, Reminders and Intimations, etc. Reports can be generated by Date as well.

DELPLUS Ver 1.0.0

Special Features

- Software is designed and developed exclusively to work in all types of libraries.
- DELPLUS is menu driven with Graphical User Interface (GUI). It is a user-friendly tool.
- It has an effective administration and security system and provides for password both for system Administrator as well as the User.
- Follows internationally recommended formats such as MARC-21, US MARC and CCF.
- Best for smaller libraries which have collections up to one lakh holdings.
- Barcode enabled
- Reservation facility for materials.
- Online monitoring of the status of material.
- Interactive facility for maintaining library inventoryl-database.
- Generation of reminders and intimations to the Members.
- Generation of reminders to vendorlsupplierlbinder, etc.
- Advanced backup and recovery system
- Online listing of country and language information with related codes.
- Online Help system for all modules.

This software comprises Acquisition, Cataloguing, Circulation, OPAC Search, Article Indexing, Authority Control Systems, and System Administration modules.

Granthalaya

Granthalaya is an integrated software package for library Information systems designed specifically to meet all needs of general as well as special libraries by Ananth Technologies Pvt Ltd of Hyderabad. It handles large, text-intensive and unlimited number of records and provides fast access on free text searches and eases the tasks of acquisition, cataloguing, circulation and information management. It is a friendly package to both the librarians and users. It has been developed using the most advanced technologies and tools like Visual Basic HTML, DHTML, ASP and JavaScript and VBScript to make the application platform independent and portable to web browsers. It is also compatible with Oracle, MS-SQL Server, MS-Access, etc., and is available for both single user and multi user environments.

Administration Module

It designed to create a database of unlimited number of bibliographic records on all formats of library material. This module enables libraries in book acquisition and serial control. It facilitates pre-order searching of books, the orders against available books, generation of notices to the overdue and incomplete supplies, budget allocation and status of funds available under different heads, calculation of actual and committed expenses with appropriate currency conversions, generation of accession register, etc.

Circulation Module

This module maintains and updates membership records. It checks the borrowers with their photo Identify through bar code scanning and prompts their loan status. It produces lists on loan, books due for return, facilitates reservation of titles, prompts over due books, calculates fines and automatically generates notices to the borrowers.

OPAC

The data is fully protected from the users of OPAC terminals. The module facilitates members to search Library material, based on Title, Author, Subject, Language, Key words, Accession No., Publisher, Publishing Place and Year of Publication; supports bar code scanning, photo identity, and interface with Weblinternet besides generation of a number of reports Utilities Module facilitates the library staff to arrange the activities such as Binding, Photocopying, Translation, etc. Report on work status, periodical reports on various activities can also be taken. Stock verification possible through bar code scanner or manual entry. Web Enquiry allows access from the desktops to the Library and search for the Books, Articles, Journals. Demands for New BookslJournals/Audio and Video equipment to library can also be submitted from desktops.

LibEra

LibEra is an integrated library software product from Modelsoft Ltd, Hyderabad. LibEra has been designed from the beginning to be web-enabled. It provides multi-lingual support. It is a comprehensive solution for all kinds of libraries. It covers all basic modules. Its features include:

- It is platform independent; handles multiple libraries in an organisation and virtual keyboards.
- Adheres to international standards like MARC21, AACR2R, IS0 2709 and 239.50 v1995.
- Multiple security; specific features are authorised to the members; provides high security for data.
- Library members are continuously sent information through automatic, system-generated e-mails
- Provision for usage of wild cards and keywords in enquiry.
- Maintains SDI profiles of the entire members and users are informed about new arrivals in the library through mails.
- Users can customise the look and feel of their screens.
- Client machines only need to have a browser to access the package.

Acquisitions supports placing requests for new books, approvals from book suppliers, placing orders, recording invoices and other miscellaneous activities. Request for new books can placed through Internet. Periodicals supports subscription receiving, renewal, binding and other miscellaneous activities. Electronic storage supports adding, viewing, modification of electronic storage. It also supports disposal of expired and damaged storage. Cataloguing helps in cataloguing of books that enter the library through acquisitions, approvals, gifts, loans or any other means. Enquiry may be accessed through Internet.

This feature helps in enquiry on books, periodicals and electronic storage. Circulation supports issue, receive, renewal, lost, reservation and lending books and periodicals. Administration helps in administering the whole system. It defines how the whole system should work. Here new users, suppliers and agents can be created; billing configurations, currency conversion rates, subjects, categories, designations, SDI profiles can be configured from here. Gazette management helps you in management of Gazettes (Government order). This also helps in maintainance of information bank of newspaper articles.

Librarian Suite

Developed by Soft-Aid Computers Ltd, Pune, the software contains four subsystems, *viz.*, Librarian for integrated library management functions; Librarian Q&A, online public access catalogue; Dossier for journal article indexing, archival and retrieval; and Librarian on Web for Internetllntranet ASP-based querying. The software is capable of working on DOS, Unix and Windows platforms including Windows NT. It can handle more than 2 lakh records and is available in multi-lingual format. It can also handle user-defined media. It is installed in some R&D, banking and public sector institutions.

LibSys

It is a fully integrated library management system developed by LibSys Corporation, New Delhi. It is a multi-user system capable of running on DOS, Unix, Xenix, VMS, and Windows platforms. It can be customised to suit the user needs and can be operated with other RDBMS software such as Ingress and Oracle. The LibSys 4 developed in C language is a client server implementation and provides ample flexibility in choosing operating platforms. It supports all Unix, Windows NT, Novell NetWare environments and provides graphical user interface on client side.

There are options for various MARC formats and CCF. It follows ANSI 2.39.50 protocol for bibliographic search. It can handle images and multimedia. Besides the library house keeping operations, it supports article indexing, abstracts and generating CAS, SDI and bibliographies with full editing features. It has powerful search engine and Web interface for Internetllntranet applications, options to have back-end RDBMS such as Oracle, or MS SQL. Libraries of various public and private organisations, scientific laboratories, universities and colleges and public libraries in India use LibSys package. The LibSys software has been in operation since 1988. There are over 600 sites in different user segments through out the country besides British Council Libraries (in South-Asian region) as well as a couple of Central American clients use the software.

Many organisations have taken multiple site license of the software which include British Council Libraries, Department of Space, CSIR, ICAR, Indian Oil Corporation, llMs and IITs. Acquisition Module covers initiation of titles for ordering with options to import data to download from network or enter data including checking for duplication; placing of orders; invoice processing; accessioning; order follow-up; receiving and accessioning of free and gift items are also dealt with online queries may be made on titles, orders, invoices, vendors, and budget heads; and corresponding reports can be printed. Various reports such as approval request form, purchase orders, overdue notices, budget and expenditure analysis, payment requisition report, accession register, and bill register can be generated and printed on requirement. Cataloguing Module maintains a titles in-process file of all items that are accessioned.

This system covers catalogue maintenance, thesaurus construction; authority files; and holdings updates. Holding summary by a range of call numbers, and 3×5 catalog cards can be printed. It provides the facility to provide Current

Awareness Services such as SDI, special bibliographies, and lists of recent arrivals. It makes possible importlexport of bibliographic data in both MARC and non-March formats; and automates the stock verification process Circulation Module supports issue and returns, renewals, reservations and membership registration; generated and print barcoded ID Cards with the members photograph; titles on display; in circulation, and in bindery; overdue follow-up and recall facility; inter-library loans and stock verification; Query and reports facilities cover a range of statistics on both borrowers and collection, including highly reserved titles, non-circulating material, number of checkins by titlelborrower, delinquency cases, etc. The system keeps a complete log of all circulation transactions.

Serials Module provides for new subscription;renewal; invoice processing; budget and expenditure analysis (Kardex update); claims monitoring (including generating notices for issues 'not receiver', overdue, or received in a damaged condition); bindery management; recording and accessioning bound volumes; online queries on various aspects of serial control including the holdings and circulation of all periodicals. OPAC provides access to the library holdings through various catalogues and indexes such as author, title, subject, and classified catalogue, publishers' index, conference place index and KWICIKWOC indexes. Also possible are combination searches using Boolean operators that yield highly satisfying and precise results, however complex the query. OPAC also provides the facility to request acquisition of titles, to reserve materials; and to send personalised SDI, overduelrecalllcollect notices and messages by e-mail.

Web OPAC provides and advanced GUI to enable searching of the library database through an industry standard web browser such as Netscape, internet Explorer, etc. Article Indexing facilitates indexing and abstracting of articles from various journals in a separate database. It includes scanning of articles, entry of citation, online searches on author, keywords1 descriptors and even word-based free text searches. This system also provides periodic documentation lists, personalised SDI, bibliographies on specific subjects, etc.

Maitrayee

Developed for use in the CALIBNET by the CMC Ltd, Secunderabad, *Maitrayee* facilitates library computerisation, resource sharing, standardisation, connectivity and modularity. The project was funded by NISSAT. It has been developed on Ingress RDBMS supported by Unix platform. It is compatible with 180-2709 and conversion from CCF to UNIMARC or vice versa is possible. Other features like bar code reading and OCR are incorporated. Apart from routine library operations the software facilitates central host and networking services including supporting protocols like TCPIIP and X.25.

PALMS and CLMSZ

Prasad Automated Library Management Systems (PALMS) and Computerised Library Management Systems version 2 (CLMS2) are developed and distributed by the Nutan Software and Publishing, Almora. Both the software packages support most of the library routines and data conversions. They are Y2K complaint, compatible with dBase, FoxPro and word processing languages for report generation. PALMS also supports CAS, SDI and bibliographical services. Both the packages are modestly priced and are within the reach of small and medium-sized libraries.

Sanjay

Sanjay is developed by DESIDOC and is marketed by NISSAT. This package is an extension of CDSIISIS capabilities through the PASCAL interface. It has a set of 70 Pascal programmes and 25 special menus. It has a faster response time - 1 minute for a query on 12,000 documents. It interlinks effectively two or more databases and also handles numeric calculations.

It is user-friendly for library housekeeping operations. *Sanjay* is based on CDSIISIS ver 2.3. It is capable of interlinking two or more databases, handling numerical calculations and other house keeping operations. The salient features of the package include Maintenance Module, User Module,

Circulation Module and Online Catalogue Module. The Maintenance Module restricts the access rights as authorised by the Database Administrator.

For data security and for providing selective access, the Maintenance Module is accessible to authorised users only. The User Module helps the library staff to carry out daily routine and assist the library users in circulation control, acquisition control, online catalogue and serials control. The Online Catalogue Module is interlinked to the circulation, acquisition and cataloguing activities. The major databases linked by it include books database, members database, acquisition database, vendors database, budget database and serials database. Any standard PC available nowadays can be used to run this software.

SLIM++

System for Library Information Management (SLIM) is a library software package from Algorithms, Pune. SLIM++ is an integrated, multi-user, multitasking library information software for the Windows environment. It helps the librarian catalogue books, firms, sound recordings, drawings, clippings, articles, reports, letters, pamphlets, serials publications, etc. SLIM++ cataloguing adheres to popular international standards. One can share data with others effectively. Retrieval of the data is simple, fast and efficient. It has Cataloguing, Circulation OPAC, Acquisition Serials Control, Web Based OPAC, Bulletin Printing (CAS), Statistical Analysis, Exportllmport in CCFIMARC, DBridge, 239.50 server modules. SLlM is widely used by many schools, colleges, research institutes, public libraries, corporate houses, etc.

SLlM is upgraded continuously to meet the technological advances in the field of data storage, retrieval, user interaction and communications. SLIM++, highly revised version, has been introduced in May 2001. SLIM++ is user friendly, menu driven, and highly interactive software. To operate SLlM no prior knowledge of computers is required. On-site training and high quality reference manuals ensure smooth transition from the current computerised or manual system to SLIM.

General Features:

- Minimal data entry, pick-up lists during data entry, validation and integrity checks
- Bar code support with multimedia links
- Browsing your library information through the Internetllntranet
- Multi-script/multi-fonts
- Variable length fieldslrecords, Packinglpurging records
- Existing data conversion to SLIM++
- Optional customised retrospective data entry and data capture
- Multiple selection criteria for reports

Windows Features:

- Adherence to Windows standards with menu bar, taskbar, window resising, window moving, multitasking using simultaneous operations in multiple windows.
- Point and click reduces users learning curve.
- Drag and drop, cut and paste reduce data entry efforts and increases uniformity and accuracy of the data.
- Wizard mode for beginners; to formulate search query, users need not remember steps.
- Online help/tool tips.
- Use of Windows standards dialogues for saving, opening and search in.
- Use of rich text format for user specified fonts, colours and sizes.
- Multi-media links to drawings, sounds, scanned files, web sites, etc.
- Interface with standards Windows applications like Wordpad, MS-Word, Mail Exchangers, etc.

SOUL

University libraries are complex entities, having large collections and serving a huge clientele. To carry out various operations in a university library effectively, there is a need for automation. Keeping in view the latest trends in information technology, INFLIBNET Center has developed a Windows-based library management software SOUL (Software for University Libraries), which provides total solution for library automation. SOUL is designed using client-server architecture, which imparts extra strength to storage capacity, multiple access to single database, various levels of security, back up, and storage facilities, etc. This software has been designed after a comprehensive study of different library-related functions practiced in university libraries.

It has MS-SQL Server 6.5 RDBMS as the back end. This user-friendly software is quite easy to work with. The software comprises Acquisition, Catalogue, Circulation, OPAC, Serial Control, and Administration modules. The in-built network feature of the software will allow multiple libraries of the same university to function together as well as access to the distributed databases installed at various university libraries and union catalogue mounted at INFLIBNET using VSAT network. Other features include availablity at nominal cost to university libraries, software designed and developed exclusively to work under university environment, network feature of the software will allow multiple libraries of university to function together, exhaustive training at INFLIBNET supported by comprehensive manual, on-site training and free updation/modification, free technical assistance and following standard formats such as CCF, AACR2, and LCSH.

Acquisition

The Acquisition module enables library staff to handle major functions related to acquisition of library material including Suggestions management, Ordering cancellation and reminders, Receiving, Payment including fund control, Master file management such as currency table, vendors, publisher, user, etc. Through this module library staff can search the entire database of library holdings for the purpose of duplicate check, etc. Using various combinations, number of reports could be generated.

Catalogue

This module is used for retrospective conversion of books, technical processing of books received from Acquisition Section, printing a range of records for verification, searching by title and accession numbers, authority files for publishers, etc. One of the unique features of SOUL is accessing to authority files on screen as well as selection box in various fields of records. Once the proposed VSAT Network by INFLIBNET is commissioned this module will take care of automatic replication of data into union catalogue. This will avoid exchange of library data on physical media, *i.e.*, floppy, tape, etc. This module covers Cataloguing Process, Catalogue Search, User Services, Catalogue card generation, Authority file maintenance, Retro conversion, Stock verification, Report Generation, Union database maintenance (local level), and Exportllmport of records.

Circulation

This module will take care of all possible functions dealt in a university library setup. Starting from membership management, maintenance of status of library items can be handled using SOUL. The circulation transactions, *viz.*, issue, return, renewal, reserve, recall, hold can be successfully done. The complex functions like fine management for each category of user and material-wise can also be effectively managed. Inter library loan, searching the status of every member or library item is possible. Reminders for overdue material, generation of various reports have also been covered.

OPAC

The Online Public Access Catalogue (OPAC) of SOUL is a window to the library collection. Using the user friendly menus, user can search for an item available in the library by author, title, corporate author, conference name, subject descriptors, class number, etc. The Boolean search enables the user to conduct the search using all combinations including type of material, language, year, etc. Besides, this will serve as first point of information about the library and also gateway for accessing INTERNET, union databases, or any other external sources.

Serial Control

The complex job of keeping track of serials can easily and effectively be handled using SOUL through its Serial Control module. This module broadly handles Suggestions, Subscription (renewal and new subscription), Payment including fund control, etc., Check in of issues including prediction of issues arrival, Reminder generation, Binding management, Search status of every item, Master database management, Reports generation, etc. User administration facility module is used for creating new users and giving them right for accessing different modules.

Suchika

It is an integrated software package, exclusively developed by DESIDOC for use by the Defence Science Library (of DESIDOC) and other librariesltechnical information centres of the Defence R&D Organisation (DRDO). One of the objectives was to follow uniform standards for creating Holdings Database of DRDO Libraries and to help automate the DRDO libraries. Initially, *Suchika* was developed in C++ language on MS-DOS and Unix, and version 2 on Windows NT platform. The software conforms the CCF, AACRZ and 180-2709 and allows data conversion from CDS/ISIS, dBase and FoxPro through application programmes. It is Y2K complaint. The software has powerful search facilities.

Suchika version 2 offers many new facilities over the previous version. Apart from Y2K compliance and supporting all library routines, the software has capabilities to interface with Webllnternet. One can search the OPAC, which is hosted on the Web, and download information. Alternatively, DESIDOC can send downloaded files (against a query) through e-mail, which is provided for in Suchika version 2. Another unique feature is adding titles and abstracts of serials received to generate CAS, SDI, Current Additions (books and periodicals) and generating catalogue of bound volumes (for individual libraries) or union catalogue (for a group of libraries). The databases can be converted to CD-ROM. It facilitates duplicate checking also. Comtek Computers Pvt. Ltd., the developer (for DESIDOC) of Suchika, markets a variant of this software under the trade name Troodon.

Virtua ILS

Virtua Integrated Library System is a comprehensive, integrated library software package from VTLS Inc, Virginia, USA. It has the modules of Acquisition and Fund Management, Circulation, Cataloging, Serials Control, etc. There are several features that are unique to VTLS Virtua ILS.

- It is fully parameterised software: User library can configure the setting to its maximum flexibility.
- It adopts UNICODE and as a result can support number of language fonts not normally supported by others.
- ILS has 239.0 built into the software. As a result, ILS users can reach external library catalogs easily and conduct searches. Converse is also true, if other libraries permit access to reach external databases.
- There is a powerful language editor to input records in different languages.
- It has provision for RFlD tags and labels
- It comes with a Chameleon Gateway: With the help of this gateway, the user's screen can be customised according to his needs.
- It has an exhaustive statistics and reporting module.
- It comes with heavy security possibilities: Security of access can be monitored at user, user Group, patron, patron group and location library levels. Depending upon security rights granted to you, the tool bar on your screen contains only those icons that are usable by you.

A *Note on RFlD Technology*

RFlD stands for Radio Frequency Identification. labels, which are as thin as paper, contain electronic chip, embedded with details of the patron, accession number of a book, etc. These are pasted onto books, user's cards, etc. RFID sensing devices 'read' these RFlD labels or Tags remotely from a distance, that is, no line of sight positioning of the reader is needed. As a result, a number of advantages arise.

- Stock verification and inventory control could be carried out using hand held reading devices. Just wave the reader across the shelf, all accession numbers are read in.
- Theft detection is possible if a reader is fitted to the exit door. When a user unauthorisedly takes out a book, RFlD scanner detects it and raises an alarm.
- Unmanned self-service counters can be maintained for checking in and checking out books. After scanning incoming books, software automatically "cancels" the issue.
- Identification of misplaced items will become easy.
- Greater availability of books because wrong shelving can be avoided and corrected.
- It leads to greater efficiency and productivity in library.

New Hanovar County Public Library in North Carolina has started using RFlD technology from January 2001. In Hyderabad, the Central University of Hyderabad has procured Virtua ILS for automating their Digital Library.

DEVELOPMENT OF DATABASES

Although database industry in India is of recent origin, it had roots in 1970s when India participated actively in many international database initiatives, especially those promoted by the UN like INIS, AGRIS and FOSTIS. In addition, many of the libraries and information centres in the S&T, research and academic institutions have been using both printed and online versions of foreign bibliographic databases since more than a decade.

However, serious efforts in the development of bibliographic databases in the country were started only in the late 1980s. INSDOC and NASSDOC took initiative in this direction with the development of National Union Catalogue of Scientific Serials in India (NUCSS I) and Union Catalogue of Social Science Periodicals, respectively.

During this period, NISSAT provided thrust to the development of indigenous databases on machine tools, leather, food, drugs and pharmaceuticals, textiles, chemicals, and ceramics. In recent times, DESIDOC took active role in the development of market for the creation of bibliographic databases. Largely due to its role of training the trainers, many institutions, especially professional associations in New Delhi, were able to develop expertise in taking up bibliographic database creation projects. Various factors which led to the interest in the databases in the country include:

- The government's liberalisation policies which led to an awareness of information as an indispensable resource for industrial growth,
- Gpenetration of computers in every sphere of activity, and
- The introduction and popularisation of various information services and products like online services, bulletin boards, and value added reports.

An international conference on the subject was organised by DESIDOC, which has provided momentum to these efforts. In 1990, a publication brought out by the National Management Information System (NMIS) of DST listed 89 databases in S&T developed by 58 government, public and private sector agencies. A majority of these databases were in computerised form, with a few in non-computerised form. The recent Indian Abstracting and Indexing Services and Databases in Science and Technology (INDAB2) compiled by NISSAT lists 398 entries, an increase of 105 entries over the earlier edition. All the 113 databases, 45 out of 202 abstracting and indexing (A&I) services and 43 out of 83 directories are machine-readable databases.

In all there were 201 machine-readable databases. These databases are developed/produced by as many as 177 agencies, which include 38 government departments, 72 R&D organisations, 48 academic institutions and universities, and

19 from private sector. However, most of the databases (more than 80 per cent) fall in science and technology and the rest are in social sciences, management, business, industry, etc. Some of these databases are available on CD-ROM.

Only one is available through international vendors. At present financial and business information is the focus of many successful commercial database developers and databases for merchant bankers, investors, corporate entrepreneurs, and financial analysts dominate the commercial scene with a couple of databases being provided online (for example, JURIX and BISNET). It is expected that the trend is likely to improve further in the next decade. Many databases are the result of transformation from print form to floppy diskettes, which now are slowly migrating to CD-ROMs.

BISNET

The Business Information System Network (BISNET) of the Federation of Indian Chambers of Commerce and Industry (FICCI) focuses on Indian business and industry. It provides comprehensive information on government policies, domestic and foreign business news, industry profiles, bibliographic database of books and journals, and the Kompass India Business Directory comprising 70,000 addresses. Online access is provided through PSTN lines or I-Net.

CIMM

The Corporate Information on Magnetic Medium (CIMM) service of the Centre for Monitoring Indian Economy (CMIE) provides access to information on economic intelligence, Indian economy and industry. CMIE possess voluminous databases running to a few GB. The databases are also accessible through Dialog.

DataServe of BI Infotech

A subsidiary of Business India group, offers databases related to stock market, foreign exchange, money and commodity markets, and other general interest databases like Business India, Express Computer, Computer Mart, etc. These databases are available through I-Net. On subscription, one can access these databases, as well as use the e-mail service, aXcess which in turn can reach Internet e-mail addresses. DataServe has a subscriber base of more than 3000 and around 10,000 e-mail users.

India Online

A subsidiary of Dataline and Research Technologies (India) Ltd. (DART), it offers e-mail under the brand name DARTMAIL. India Online has its own network linking Ahmedabad, Bangalore, Calcutta, Chennai, Delhi, Hyderabad, Mangalore and Mumbai. It provides real-time access to corporate financial and performance data of about 5000 companies. The database is also available on CD-ROM with monthly updates. It also provides access to external databases like the legal database, JURIX.

Informatics India (P) Ltd

The Bangalore-based firm is one of the most successful firms offering library services including databases of Dialog. The firm has been supplying the CD-ROM databases of Silver Platter. Of late it started mastering and producing databases on CD-ROM, using the WinSPIRS retrieval software of Silver latter. The firm produced many databases on CD-ROM, on turnkey basis. Some of them are MTec on CD database for the Central Manufacturing Technology Institute, Catalogue of DRDO Holdings (on CD) for DESIDOC and the Indian Business Inside Database (IBID) on CD.

Legal Databases

JURIX, India's legal database, covers Civil Procedure Code, legislative acts like, Arbitration Act, Company Acts, Excise and Customs Acts, Transfer of Proprietary Act, High Court and Supreme Court decisions on direct taxes, and MRTP Case Laws. There are 12 databases, most of which cover information from 1981. It is available online with user-friendly search software through India Online. The Judgement Information System (JUDIS) is an online database of case law information for judges, lawyers, law students, libraries and the litigants. The database, part of the Court Information System (COURTIS) offered by the NIC, is accessible by NICNET terminals in all the district headquarters.

ADVANTAGES OF LIBRARY AUTOMATION

Many activities of a library are routine in nature; a few are repetitive. Automation of these activities helps in managing the library's resources in a better way at the same time saving time, money and manpower. For example, once the bibliographic details like author, title, edition, publisher, price, ISBN number, etc are entered at the time of ordering, the same data can be used for accessioning, cataloguing (OPAC), and circulation. Other important factors associated with automation are speed, and accuracy.

One can imagine the time saved in literature searches and in preparing bibliographies. Automation also offers freedom from doing repetitive and routine works as well as enables providing efficient services properly and more efficiently cutting down time and improving productivity Automation also facilitates generation of a number of reports for better decision making in the effective management of the library. Availability of various statistical and other usage reports and performance reports will ensure better appreciation from library users.

For example, vendor performance analysis is possible. Subject-wise or project/department-wise budget can be monitored. Circulation data can provide information on titles that are in great demand so that more copies can be procured if needed. Many current awareness services like current additions, contents of books and journals, etc can also be provided to users.

2

Library Automation and Organisational Change

The University Libraries of Notre Dame closed their library system, NOTIS, during Christmas break in 1998. In January of 1999, they brought a new library system, Aleph, into production. The NOTIS system is based on a large IBM mainframe with text-based terminals. Library patrons and staff use the same terminal connections to access the catalog. The system is command driven, and all computation activity takes place on the mainframe.

Aleph is a client-server system, using an ORACLE database mounted on a UNIX server. The library staff use a Windows client on PCs to access the database. This client uses a graphical interface, with drop-down menus and buttons. Staff edit records on PCs, and send them back to the server when they are finished. The library patrons do not use the same software to access the catalog. Instead, they connect with their web-browsers, using virtually any computer platform they like.

IDENTIFICATION OF THE ISSUE

The example is only one instance of the large-scale changes that affect people's work lives. These types of changes raise many important issues for managers, from the level of director to unit supervisor. Some issues are primarily technological. What equipment will be needed? Is the technological infrastructure in place? Will the system crash when the date changes to January 1, 2000? Other issues are more social. How will the employees react? Will they accept the change or resist it? Can the change process be made easier? Unfortunately, this second group of issues can be easily overlooked. Managers often do not address human issues adequately, even though they are aware of them, and even though they consider their employees, clients, and other people to be important (Backer).

CHANGE ISSUES IN THE PUBLIC AND PRIVATE SECTORS

While the specific issue of library automation is located principally in the public sector, the processes and challenges of change are common to both areas.

HUMAN FACTORS IN LIBRARY AUTOMATION

Librarians, staff and patrons must make a number of adjustments as a result of any library automation project, whether it is an original implementation or a migration. One key area is the relationship between people and technology. People have to change the way they behave and think to work effectively in an automated environment. They skim through cards to find a catalog record in a manual system. To find a catalog record in an automated system they use computer commands.

In a migration scenario, this might be a change from typing keyboard commands to choosing buttons or menu items on a graphical interface. For long-term employees, this requires yet a third "mental map." These demands for change easily lead to stress reactions of fear or anger, especially when they are large-scale or frequent. Smith mentions several sources for these emotions, such as loss of control, worries about identity and security in the workplace, and breakdowns in interpersonal relationships. It is no wonder that people often resist change.

However, researcher cautions against regarding human responses solely as a barrier to change. For leaders who pay attention to social issues, these responses provide valuable feedback and help to implement a more successful system.

HISTORICAL PERSPECTIVE

The early history of library automation can be divided into three phases, the Developmental Phase, the Operational Phase, and the Integrative Phase (Montague). The development phase was the period of early experimentation up to the early seventies. During this period a small number of institutions engaged in automation projects. While management hoped that systems could be transferred from one institution to another, this was not the case with these early efforts. Libraries did not have similar computer operating systems, they did not have standardised procedures, and they could not agree on outputs.

However, the development of the MARC record was a significant development that allowed libraries to communicate bibliographic records in a standard format. The operational phase, in the mid-to-late seventies, saw the expansion of automation in a wider variety of libraries. Vendor-supplied systems, shared computer resources, and networking made this possible. Since libraries were no longer forced to develop their own systems from scratch, it was an easier and less expensive task. During this phase most library automation projects still focused on discrete tasks, such as check-in or circulation.

Operational areas were not integrated, and the overall workflow stayed basically the same, "it has been utterly possible to use the automated system as inefficiently and ineffectively and with as little knowledge of what is going on as with the manual system" (Montague). Montague proposed that the next phase would be an integrative phase, in which the automation systems would cut across operational lines, actually change the way libraries do business, and improve service.

There were a number of obstacles during these stages of library automation:

- Lack of direction and oversight from library managers to systems staff
- Lack of technical training for library managers
- Failure to develop long-range plans (including a cost

analysis of the manual systems and the automated replacements)

- Lack of up and down communication between managers and staff
- Lack of staff input
- Lack of staff training
- Lack of feedback mechanisms

Overall, it appears that the several problems, training, oversight, input, feedback, all involved a general lack of communication.

MIGRATION: SECOND GENERATION SYSTEMS

Since many libraries, including Notre Dame, have or plan to migrate to second generation library systems, it is important to consider whether the obstacles are the same. One view (representing a system vendor) is that they are not the same. Migrations are said to be easier than initial implementations. Although there may be some staff apprehensions, staff morale is reported to improve. A significant advantage is that second-time buyers have a better understanding of what they want in a system, and focus more on quality and customer support, instead of low bids.

There is one potential source of resistance, which is never present in an initial automation project, that is a hostile "soon-to-be former vendor." Another important distinction is whether the library is migrating after successful implementation of a system which simply no longer meets their needs, or whether the library is desperately seeking a new system after a failed effort (Sybrowsky). The reaction of librarians to this viewpoint is to be mixed. Some libraries have reported a very similar degree of "technostress" during migration projects, with similar emotional responses (stress, fear and anxiety).

Staff are required to change procedures, and in many cases the new procedures are not clear-cut — of course, the procedures in the "old" system were not clear-cut in the beginning either (Saunders). On the other hand, the majority of directors in a survey of 33 libraries that had undergone system migrations felt that "promoting" the system change to the staff was unnecessary. This seems to be primarily due to staff frustration with the old systems, providing a clear motivation for change. The worse the original system, the less staff resistance there was to migration.

However, there were still some symptoms of technostress. Many found the vendors training programmes to be inadequate, consisting of "canned" presentations were did not apply to local needs. Due to "rush jobs," the staff at many libraries did not have adequate time to become familiar with the new system before it was made available to the public. In one particularly egregious case, the staff and patrons were given access to the system at the same time. The staff "hated this." A two-month lead-time between staff and public access gave optimum results (Hallmark).

PRIVATE SECTOR EXPERIENCES

While library automation, *per se*, is not a major issue in the for-profit world, automation in general definitely is. As such, experiences in the private sector provide helpful comparisons. One very familiar theme from corporate settings in the need to consult with users prior to any sort of migration or automation project. This is true even with systems that are not central to the users' jobs. Gaudin relates several stories of companies that tried to implement new systems without consulting users.

One case involved replacing a mainframe e-mail system with a desktop system. After the company spent $3 million, the employees rejected it because it was not fast or stable enough. In another case, FedEx introduced a scheduling system (which had been very popular with employees at *other* airlines) without consulting their *own* employees. This became one of the issues in a potential strike against the company. One manager pointed out the importance of remembering that "users might like their old systems".

This is an important lesson for library managers to remember in a migration, especially when the original system was basically successful. Even a failed system may have features the employees liked. Another illustration is provided by Norman's study of a failed automation effort. An attempt to introduce the CASE (computer-aided software engineering) system in a management information firm provides valuable lessons for both sectors. The goal of the CASE project was to establish a 2-1 ratio of CASE workstation usage among the MIS staff and achieve a 10 to 15 per cent increase in productivity. The project is considered to be a failure, because people are not using it.

The company has lost business to competitors who do use the system. Researcher identifies a number of factors in the CASE implementation, which contributed to its failure. From the beginning, the decision to implement CASE was made by a small high-level committee, without involving staff. There was a successful pilot project, following which the company attempted to expand the system. Their main methodology was a staff-training programme. Management assumed that if they provided training, the programmers would use the system. While the training was described as "adequate," it was informational only, and there was no effort made to change attitudes.

The most critical barrier identified in the study was the high learning curve for using CASE. Management did not make any effort to reduce this learning curve. Instead, each work group that attempted to use the system had to learn it on their own. There was no sharing of tricks or shortcuts, or any help given by those who had already started using the product to new users. Interdepartmental friction and a rigid chain-of-command that stifled communication between units prevented this type of cooperation.

A related factor was the lack of any visible benefits or rewards for using CASE. Instead rewards were based on completing projects under-time and under-budget. Since CASE is intended to increase productivity, it might seem that this would reward its use. But "this means that the rewards are indirect and totally dependent upon the *successful* use of the tool" (Norman, emphasis added). In conjunction with the high learning curve, this becomes a negative incentive – the system is likely to slow production in the short-term, until the learning curve is past. If the programmer fails to learn it quickly, rewards are lost rather than gained.

THEORIES AND STRATEGIES FOR CHANGE

In discussing theories of organisational change, many theorists divide changes into different types. Before delving too deeply into specific strategies for change, I would like to examine the relationship between library automation projects and descriptive theories. Continuity In the Age of Unreason, Handy tells us that "Change is not what it used to be". He distinguishes continuous and discontinuous change. Continuous change is gradual and predictable, with one situation leading into the next. This is relatively comfortable for most people. But he asserts that the changes in the workplace now (and in life in general) are discontinuous. That is, changes are abrupt and unpredictable, and hence, far less comfortable.

Handy frequently links discontinuous change to technology. As such, it is easy to reach the conclusion that a library automation project is a discontinuous change. People who worked with paper switch to online systems, and their jobs are altered or even eliminated. But we should not be too quick to classify it this way. Particularly in the early automation projects, automated tasks were substituted for manual tasks on a one-to-one basis. Because of this, there was no drastic change in the overall workflow; even when specific tasks were drastically altered (Montague). It could be argued that automation has had a more significant impact since that time, as library systems have become integrated.

CALM AND TURBULENT WATERS

Robbins focuses on the frequency of change. He uses two metaphors, "calm waters" and "whitewater rapids." In the calm-waters scenario, change is the exception. Most of the time is spent in a state of equilibrium, until some crisis (the storm) forces a change. After the change is past, the organisation regains a new (albeit different) state of equilibrium. In the white-water scenario, change is continuous, though in a different sense than Handy uses the word. There is no state of equilibrium; instead one period of change is followed directly by another.

It is very tempting to identify library automation projects with the "calm water" metaphor. In fact, Saunders uses a very similar model in her article on library system migration. First various forces bring about a need for change, which requires unfreesing process. This is followed by a period of instability (the actual time of the change). When this is over, the library establishes a new state of equilibrium, as new patterns and procedures are frozen into place. Because automation efforts are not made frequently, this model appears to be a good match. In an original automation project, the library has been using a manual system as long as it has been in existence. Once the project has been completed, the library will continue to use the new system indefinitely.

Even in a migration project, the library may have been using its old system for many years, and certainly would hope the new system would be long-lived. One potential problem with this model is that it ignores the wider picture of overall changes. At the same time as a library is contemplating an integrated library system, the staff may be dealing with new (and ever-changing) online indexes, electronic journals, e-mail systems, computer operating systems, and even (in Notre Dame's case) a building renovation. Taken in this larger context, the white water metaphor seems more appropriate to the library environment.

It is often not just the project at hand that causes problems for staff and users, but the "unrelenting demand" of changes in many areas. Another issue is the continuing change following the implementation of an automated system due to new releases and upgrades to the system. Even after a new system is fully implemented, it may not be as "calm" as the old manual system. One significant problem with the white-water model as a model for change is that it suggests a reactive style of management with unplanned changes. But most library automation and migration projects are planned, as are many (not all) of the other changes affecting the library staff.

This model seems most apt for dealing with the external changes impacting an organisation.

THE FOUR MOTORS OF CHANGE

Van de Ven and Poole give a more fully fleshed taxonomy of change. They identify two crosscutting distinctions, the level and the mode of change. The level of change is whether the change involves single or multiple entities (an entity being anything from an individual to an institution). The mode of change is either prescribed or emergent. *A priori* changes are planned, predictable or follow set rules or patterns (what Handy would describe as continuous). Emergent change is discontinuous and unpredictable. This combination yields four "motors of change."

- Life-cycle (single entity, prescribed)
- Teleological (single entity, emergent)
- Dialectical (multiple entities, emergent)
- Evolutionary (multiple entities, prescribed)

While these motors can be separated in theory, most real-life changes involve interaction between them. The four motors model provides a more complete description of organisational change, and avoids oversimplification problems. If we examine library automation projects in this e context of the four motors of change that Van de Ven describes, as suggested, find rather complex interactions. The teleological theory, which is characterised by planning and goal setting, provides the closest description of the first stage in an automation project.

Libraries may have a variety of motivations for undertaking an automation or migration project. In the case of migration, this might include negative factors, like dissatisfaction with the current vendor, as well as positive ones, like a desire to expand capabilities. These motivations provide the Aristotelian final cause for the project. Most libraries engage in goal setting activities, such as compiling lists of desired features. This stage may be described as teleological in Van de Ven's scheme because it primarily involves one entity (the library) and the process is emergent. At the beginning of this stage, it is not clear where it will finish.

Although the process is planned (rather than reactive) the goals are identified during the process, and may provide a dramatic break (or discontinuity) with the existing manual or automated system. The dialectical motor may be present to a lessor extant, as different stakeholders (such as work units) interact with each other, and occasionally present conflicting goals. This teleological description fits most, but not all migration projects. For 79 per cent of cases in a migration survey, the projects were planned. But in some cases, the libraries did not have time to develop plans due to legal or financial problems. In those cases, the teleological motor would only apply in a trivial sense, if at all. Those cases are obviously not ideal scenarios.

Towards the end of the selection process, the library must compare its goals and desires to the actual systems available. At this point, the process could be described as dialectical, involving the library and the vendors who would like to supply the system. Vendors and librarians both regard this process as different for migration projects compared to first-time automation efforts. In a first-time automation, libraries tend to rely on numerical evaluation of vendors' proposals and claims. In migration projects, libraries find site visits to be the most effective way to evaluate quality and hands-on work issues.

At some point either during the final selection process or shortly after a vendor is chosen, the process shifts to a life-cycle model. The life-cycle motor is also primarily concerned with the library as a single entity. At this point, the plan, which was developed in earlier stages, becomes the guide for the process.

The library engages is a series of steps that were laid out in the plan, possibly on a strict timeschedule. This includes all of the steps technically necessary to implement the system (*e.g.*, data mapping and test conversions) as well as steps to prepare the users. This process is imminent in, or prescribed by the plan, and is much more predictable than the earlier stages. The library may have even planned for contingencies. Once the actual conversion in done, and the new system is live, the process become somewhat less predictable.

Procedures that worked on paper or in test may fail under the pressure of real-life use.

While none of the motors seem to be completely dominant at this point, the evolutionary theory is closest. Procedures that work "survive" while others are discarded. The changes may still be described as imminent, however, because they are constrained by the system. The others motors continue to play some role, as plans are made and carried out, and different stakeholders disagree on various issues. The dialectical motor may become dominant from time-to-time as the vendor announces new releases, or the library recommends enhancements for the system. At these times the possibilities for change are less constrained, and the results become more emergent.

STRATEGIES

The authors who describe actual automation projects also list key lessons and make recommendations. There are a number of general, and some very specific, suggestions along with a couple of common threads. One of the common threads is communication. Whether it is between management and employees, between systems and users, or between the employees at large, it seems that more communication is always better.

A related thread is the need to involve the users in the process as early as possible. Several of the authors suggested that users should be involved at the very beginning, during the selection process. Since these two threads stand out, we may conclude that if any overall strategy is too be effective, it must include a high level of communication and user participation.

STRATEGIES FROM THE CASE IMPLEMENTATION

Norman described three change strategies in his evaluation of the CASE implementation. These strategies could be used independently or in conjunction with each other. *Rational-empirical* This strategy focuses on training (*i.e.*, how to use the system) and information (the benefits of the system). It is presumed that teaching people to use the system and providing a rational explanation of why it is better will lead them to use it. This strategy could easily be applied to a library automation or migration project, as many of the authors indicated the importance of training programmes.

Normative-educational

This strategy focuses on group strategies for promoting acceptance of the new systems and providing motivation to use it. First, identify the attitudes that create resistance, and then develop programmes to change them. This is similar to developing training sessions in the rational-empirical strategy. The difference is that the sessions are intended to develop positive attitudes instead imparting information.

Power-coercive

In this strategy individuals are induced to use the new system by the threat of loosing their job or other benefits (*e.g.*, promotion opportunities). This can be a fairly direct approach to implement change, but it also runs a high risk creating bad feelings, job dissatisfaction, and tension between management and employees. Threats, whether explicit or implicit, will also add to the fear and anxiety already identified as an obstacle to change.

A variation of this strategy can be applied in a positive way by offering employees incentives for change. While this is can be regarded as a power-exercise (the employees who do not use the new system will not get the new benefits) it is less confrontational. In the CASE implementation, the main strategy that was applied was the rational-empirical strategy. The normative-educational strategy was largely ignored, and the power-coercive strategy was inconsistently applied. Management made statements that employees were required to use the system, but did not follow-up when it was not used. Management also did not provide any direct positive incentives. This strategy may also be applied to library systems in the sense that when the old (manual or automated) system is shut-off, employees will not be able to perform their duties without using the new system.

PHASED IMPLEMENTATION

Saunders recommends a strategy of phased implementation. The idea of this strategy is to minimize the impact of the new system has on staff by introducing modules in a gradual fashion. For example, a library might implement cataloging or acquisitions functions first, and circulation latter. This strategy has some advantages. Successful implementation of one module should increase staff willingness to use another. Also, management can deal with the staff in smaller groups, concentrating on the area currently being automated, instead of dealing with all areas at once.

The chief drawback of this strategy is found when the current system is already well integrated. In this case, phased implementation may mean that user's (staff and patrons) are initially presented with a system that has *fewer features* than their previous system. There may also be technical difficulties that preclude phased implementation, as the two systems are not likely to communicate with each other well, if at all. Where it is usable, this strategy should also be combined with other strategies. Saunders specifically emphasises the importance of training and communication issues.

PARTICIPANT ORIENTED CHANGE

Researcher advocates the strategy of participant oriented change, which is based on the premise that change works best when comes from the bottom up rather than from the top down. One reason for this premise is that if the employees introduce change, then they will not have an authority figure to rebel against. It is also based on the idea that collegial affiliation is a positive motivation for change. That is, employees will be more motivated to help with a changes initiated by someone at, or close to, their level. To use participant oriented change, management needs to shift the responsibility for change away from themselves and towards the employees.

This strategy goes beyond considering the users' needs, or soliciting input, to actually delegating authority to the participants. This strategy takes advantage of the fact that the employees who are closest to the hands-on work have the most detailed knowledge about it. This also frees the upper management from concentrating on this level of detail, and to concentrate on overall strategic planning. This strategy may not be effective in all types of organisations.

There are some essential elements for participative strategies to work. First, the employees given responsibilities for change must be well informed. Second, the employees must understand and agree with the mission of the organisation. Unless these requirements are met, management cannot expect that the decisions will be beneficial to the organisation. The third requirement is that this style of change must be supported by the organisation culture. The management must be comfortable with this type of delegation (Zeffane).

MANAGEMENT FUNCTIONS

The traditional roles of management are planning, organisation, coordination and control. These can be applied to these change strategies.

RATIONAL-EMPIRICAL

The rational-empirical strategy is primarily concerned with dispensing information, presuming that the plans for change have already been made. It involves the organising function of management, in the sense that the managers determine what information needs to be given to which employees in order to implement the changes. It also involves the control function, in that the management is seeking to influence behaviour through the information it dispenses (or withholds).

NORMATIVE-EDUCATIONAL

The normative-education strategy is concerned with influencing attitudes and behaviour. As such, it involves the control function of management, but in an indirect manner. That is, rather than controlling behaviour directly, the management attempts to instill attitudes which are likely to result in the desired behaviour. Like the rational-empirical strategy, it also involves the coordinating function, as managers decide who should be involved in which programmes.

POWER-COERCIVE

The power-coercive strategy concerns the management role of control in a straight- forward fashion. It is mainly concerned with seeing to it that the change decisions (which have already been made) are carried out as directed. To ensure this, it dispenses rewards or penalties to individuals or groups depending or whether they have implemented the changes. In the extreme, employees who fail to change are fired.

PHASED IMPLEMENTATION

Phased implementation involves both the planning and coordinating functions to a large degree. Planning includes determining the order in which to implement the modules and setting timetables for each phase. Coordination includes meshing together the efforts of different groups associated with each phase, and ensuring that each module is integrated with the previous ones when it is brought into production. As more modules are brought into the "live" mode, coordination becomes essential in order to see that the different areas function smoothly.

PARTICIPANT ORIENTED CHANGE

Participant oriented change involves the coordinating function of management. Since much of the planning and decision making is delegated downward to the staff, management must integrate these plans and decisions. This is particularly important when implementing an integrated library system (either in an initial automation, or in comparison to a less integrated system), as the activities of staff in one area will have more impact on other areas than they are accustomed to.

The actual delegation of these responsibilities to employees involves the organising function. Determining how and to whom these responsibilities are delegated is in important part of the change process. This may involve organising employees into self-managed teams, work groups, or interdepartmental task forces. How these groups are organised, the amount of authority they have, and how they will interact with each other are crucial decisions.

CONCLUSIONS AND RECOMMENDATIONS

The participant oriented change strategy provides the best overall approach to managing library automation and migration projects. Of the strategies which have been outlined, it offers the highest degree of employee communication and participation. These are the same areas that caused the most problems if they were inadequate. One of the chief advantages of this strategy is that it involves the users of the system at the earliest possible stage of the project. That is during the teleological process of identifying reasons for the project and setting goals or criteria for a new system. Involving the employees at this stage reduces the need for normative attitude-adjusting sessions latter in the process.

This is not to say that managers who adopt this strategy can just ignore employee attitudes later on. Change will still be stressful, and people may still resist it at various points. But, management will not have to invest as much effort in convincing staff that the new system is better if the staff were involved in selecting it. The rational-empirical strategies of employee training programmes will still have a role to play, as the process moves on.

As was demonstrated in the failed attempt at implementing the CASE system, this strategy is not sufficient by itself. But users must learn how a new system works if they are to use it at all. Within the overall context of participant oriented strategy, other employees provide much of that training. With their hands-on experience, employee led training can be more effective than vendorsupplied "canned presentations" (Hallmark). This also promotes an atmosphere in which employees will be comfortable sharing their learning experiences, tricks and shortcuts following implementation.

The other two strategies, phased implementation and power-coercive can not be recommended across the board. The power-coercive strategy is divisive, and is likely make the change harder instead of easier. This strategy aggravates fears about job security, which is one of the sources of change anxiety. While a degree of control needs to be maintained, a threatening approach is not desirable as a general strategy. The strategy of phased implementation will be helpful for some situations, but not for all.

For libraries currently using manual systems or automated systems that are not integrated, this method may help to ease the transition. For libraries that already have a well-integrated system, it could create even more chaos. Within the context of participant oriented change, the choice of whether to include it rests with the employees who actually work with the system.

3

Standards in Library Automation and Networking

INTRODUCTION

We live in an increasingly globalised and interconnected world. Barriers in trade, commerce, banking, industry, science, technology, education, etc., are breaking down and will continue to become more and more borderless with time. Globalisation also means increased dependency on one other in various domains. Globalisation also has increased competition; consumers of all kinds now, more than ever before, have a number of choices. Globalisation is in a sense synonymous with networking.

Computers, telecommunications infrastructure and the Internet are not only essential but indispensable in the world we live in today. The library and information world has traditionally been borderless long before others.

However, the Internet and the world wide web have pushed libraries to be even more interdependent than before, because of the bewildering array of sources and providers of information from which they draw their information. Equally, libraries are now facing competition from other players. The place of libraries as centres for the acquisition, description, organisation, preservation and access to information has been challenged by new players such as Google, Yahoo!, etc., and subject portals, digital libraries and open access repositories. These services use new methods to acquire, analyse, display and organise information and are undoubtedly a threat to the traditional role of libraries and librarians. How libraries can get an edge over competing services and continue to be relevant, different, wanted and useful has engaged the attention of many library professionals. Even before the advent of the Internet and the web, libraries sought to automate and network with each other so that their clients could have easier and wider access to resources.

The proliferation of resources such as other library catalogues, online databases, full text publications, electronic serials, learning resources, discussion forum postings, etc., on the web has posed a considerable challenge to librarians. How to cope with these new resources and newer forms of older resources is a question that requires to be addressed by all libraries. Library automation and networking, which until the 1990's was considered to be adequate, today do not provide all the answers.

Library automation and networking is all about connecting to other libraries and information centres, search engines, peer groups, databases and experts. Thus the sceanrio today is one of many dispersed digital collections. The need is to move to inter-operable digital libraries. This requires that we focus on standards of many kinds. Of these, metadata standards have assumed the highest importance. To put it in simple words, libraries and networks of all kinds use different hardware and software platforms.

To enable interconnectivity to such a diversity of systems and to enable mutual sharing of resources and exchange of data between them requires that all of them follow internationally agreed upon standards. Networks operate at different levels in respect of:

- The variety of resources they handle,
- The computer hardware they use,
- Operating system platforms,
- The language used to describe subject content,
- The support to protocols and standards they provide, and
- The back-end software in use.

The one element in all library automation and networking today that has assumed highest priority is the use of (wherever possible) international standards for the following:

- Metadata standards which includes standards for data elements as well as identification, description and representation standards;
- Information exchange standards;
- Communication standards;
- Content representation standards;
- Interoperability standards.

The categorisation is only used for convenience and it must be emphasised that there is considerable overlap in the purpose and function of these standards. It is important that these should be understood and used in library systems if there is to be effective automation and networking. This tutorial attempts to:

- Describe briefly the various metadata and interoperability standards, and
- Emphasise the importance of these standards when planning library automation and more importantly networking of libraries.

METADATA

Metadata may be described as having the following characteristics.

- Structured Data about data used to aid identification, description, management and location of resources
- Also may include physical resources, *e.g.*, metadata embedded in web pages

The earliest form of metadata records are 5" × 3" card catalogue records

METADATA STANDARDS

Metadata standards comprise the following types:

- Standards for data elements needed to describe different types of information objects — some well known, some new and some newer forms of existing objects,

- Library cataloguing standards such as the AACR2R and ISBD comprising rules on how to describe the data elements constituting information objects and rules for the determination and establishment of headings (or access points) (and sequence with separating symbols as in ISBD) under which the descriptive information is to be presented to catalogue users, and with the making of references to those headings.
- Standards (or languages) on how to represent the metadata in computers,
- Standards to represent subject content

THE MARC-21 BIBLIOGRAPHIC METADATA FORMAT

Records structured in the MARC-21 format are the most widely used ones in bibliographic databases. MARC-21 is a data element standard as well a standard that specifies how different data elements are recognised by a computer via numeric tags, numeric indicators and alphanumeric subfield codes. This format is ideally suited for variable length records, and to accommodate all the idiosyncrasies of bibliographic records such as the presence of a variable number of repeatable fields, presence of fields in some records and not in others. The MARC record was designed as a standard format for the exchange of bibliographic data between organisations, *e.g.*, two national libraries, a national library and other academic libraries. MARC formats exist for:

- Bibliographic data,
- Authority data and
- Holdings data.

The MARC format has undoubtedly been one of the most successful and durable metadata standards in the library environment. Most western library automation software support the MARC format for import of records into a local catalogue database (also called copy cataloguing) into their local databases. More than a billion metadata records are available in the MARC format with large national libraries such as the Library of Congress (LOC) and cooperative networks such as OCLC and RLN. Many sources of MARC-21 catalogue records are available free for use and download by other libraries worldwide. It makes good sense therefore for Indian libraries to use these resources within their library's. There are several advantages in doing this:

- The efficiency of cataloguing is greatly improed and therefore the cost of cataloguing can be considerably reduced
- Metadata imported from an authoritative MARC source ensures more completeness and accuracy in library catalogues.
- Use of authority files with MARC sources enhances the consistency of library catalogues.
- Exchange of a library's catalogue records is possible with other libraries via a common standard format.
- Moving from one integrated library management software (ILMS) to a more sophisticated one is more easily accomplished than if a library has to move from a non-standard structure to a standard one such as MARC-21.

Irrespective of how an integrated library management software (ILMS) represents its catalogue database records internally, *e.g.*, using a relational database management system (RDBMS) or as a flat file structure, it is important that the software should allow import of records from one or other MARC data source, *e.g.*, the national library or a cooperative network such as OCLC. In other words when considering library automation, it is important to examine the extent to which the The MARC format is supported by the ILMS. The MARC format has been an important element in the development of many union catalogues and for ensuring the exchange of data between and across library systems through out the world.

In fact, the MARC format is the bedrock on which global cooperative networks such as OCLC and the RLN are founded. Most Indian libraries by default do not use the MARC format in their catalogue databases. Similarly, most Indian library automation software do not provide the capability to seamlessly import and/or export records from and to the MARC format. This has led to many shortcomings. Some of these are given below:

- It is not possible to use copy cataloguing by downloading MARC-21 cataloguing data from authoritative sources such as the Library of Congress and other freely available web sources to build online catalogues.
- There is considerable duplicated effort across libraries apart from inconsistent entries in catalogues leading to difficulties in building union databases.
- Large libraries in India such as University libraries have not been able to act as providers of authoritative cataloguing data to smaller libraries, *e.g.*, colleges. Common use of the MARC format across libraries would enable such sharing.
- Indian libraries cannot participate in global cooperative networks such as OCLC and RLN. Indian intellectual input is thus not adequately represented in global databases.

Closely linked with the MARC-21 format are standards (actually rules) such as AACR2R and ISBD. ISBD is a set of rules produced by the International Federation of Library Associations (IFLA) to describe a wide range of library materials, within the context of a catalogue. ISBD defines a number of areas, *e.g.*, title and statement of responsibility, edition, material-dependent information (for example, the scale of a map or the duration of a sound recording). These rules organise the bibliographic description of an item. Librarians use the AACR2R and ISBD in conjunction with MARC.

AUTHORITY AND HOLDINGS RECORDS

It is important to emphasise that MARC-21 is a format not only for bibliographic records. MARC-21 formats exist for authority records and holdings records. Good ILMS software provide support to both these formats. There are several advantages of adhering to these formats in addition to the bibliographic formats:

- Local authority file records can be created via imports from an authoritative source such as the LoC.
- An ILMS could ensure that new entries of data are validated against the local authority data to ensure better consistency in the use of personal names, subject terms, etc.

It is high time that Indian libraries embrace the MARC format and look for software solutions that support this format if they wish to effectively contribute and benefit from networked resources within India and outside it. Equally importantly, today's ILMS should also provide crosswalks to and from other metadata standards.

DUBLIN CORE METADATA ELEMENT SCHEME (DCMES)

The emergence of a variety of new digital information objects and digital formats of traditional materials (*e.g.*, images, text, sound) required adaptations of traditional descriptive methods and this triggered the development of a metadata description scheme which would be simple and also cover a wide range of materials.

Work on defining such a metadata element scheme which later became known as the Dublin Core Metadata Element Scheme (DCMES) began in 1995 in an invitational workshop convened by the Online Computer Library Center (OCLC) and the National Center for Supercomputing Applications (NCSA), at Dublin, Ohio.

The workshop was attended by professionals from librarianship, computer science, text encoding, and related areas to advance the state of the art in the development of resource description of records for networked electronic information objects.

The inititaive, now known as the Dublin Core Metadata Intiative (DCMI) has had the benefit of consultations from specialists from many countries over the years. DCMES is now an international standard (ISO 15836:2003) and is also used as a national standard in countries such as New Zealand,

Australia, USA, and the UK among many others. Some of the other reasons for a new metadata schema for today's needs cited are:

- New types of information objects, (*e.g.*, web pages, computer programmes, discussion forum postings) require new methods of description to accurately describe their unique content.
- Increasing technological capabilities allow delivery of richer and more complex 'objects' (*e.g.*, an interactive learning object may have text, video and sound objects embedded into it). Such objects will need more complex descriptive methods.
- Search methods have changed. Users rely more and more on keywords than on field-directed searches, *e.g.*, personal name or title searches. Advanced searching, browsing, text-mining algorithms and relevance ranking are being employed in addition to the use of hyperlinking between two or more objects to ensure better search results and resource discovery.
- Users no longer feel limited to the resources of their institution or institutional network. They expect virtual access to resources wherever they may be available.
- The preservation needs of digital objects are very different from those of physical objects. Digital objects require to be monitored actively and detailed documentation about these is useful in helping to preserve these objects as compared to paper-based objects.
- Many new systems for direct use by authors and other professionals are now becoming available, *e.g.*, document management systems (DMS) and digital archives applications. These require that authors of various types of information objects should themselves create the metadata for the objects they author. A simpler scheme is called for in such situations and DCMES is an answer to such a need.

DCMES is a simple yet effective element set for describing a wide range of networked resources. The Dublin Core (DC) standard defines two levels: Basic and Qualified.

- *Basic Dublin Core* comprises fifteen elements;
- *Qualified Dublin Core* includes an additional element, Audience, as well as a group of element refinements (also called qualifiers) that refine the semantics of the elements in ways that may be useful in resource discovery.

The semantics and grammar of Dublin Core have been established by an international, cross-disciplinary group of professionals from librarianship, computer science, text encoding, the museum community, and other related fields of scholarship and practice. Most elements also have a limited set of qualifiers or refinements, attributes that may be used to further refine (not extend) the meaning of the element. Each of the elements is optional and may be repeated as many times as needed to describe an instance of a digital resource, *e.g.*, the full text of a journal article or an annual report; a digital image of an insect pest. Standard ways to refine elements have been defined by the Dublin Core Metadata Initiatitive (DCMI) and they encourage the use of encoding and controlled vocabulary schemes. A metadata scheme is expected to serve the following purposes:

- *Description of the intellectual content* (descriptive metadata) of an information object. The purpose of this metadata is to facilitate resource discovery.
- *Management of the digital file and the maintenance of a digital object*. This is especially important for successful preservation – that is to insure that it will be accessible even after the original hardware and software become obsolete.
- *Definition of the internal structure of an information object (structural metadata)*. This metadata provides the connection between the intellectual organisation of the information object and the digital representation of that organisation.
- *Provide information related to rights and use, i.e.,* the

social and legal restrictions on how the information object can be used, including copyright information, intellectual property and breeders rights, and usage guidelines (administrative metadata). Information on rights of use is important since many copyrighted digital objects have become accessible via the web.

Although Dublin Core (DC) was originally developed to describe document-like objects, DC metadata can be applied to other resources as well. Examples of the use of DC in many projects, some of which are quite unique in that they integrate text, images, videos, sound, and multimedia resources using Dublin Core as the basis for description.

APPLICATION PROFILES

The DCMES is more like a framework and allows domain-specific extensions. In other words, an information agency that needs to describe resources in a specific domain need not re-invent metadata elements. They can use the basic elements, the element refinements of the DCMES and add domain specific extensions together with content rules, encoding schemes and controlled vocabularies. These domain-specific schemes also have come to be known as schemas or Application Profiles.

The use of DCMES as the underlying basis of different metadata schemas or Application Profiles (AP) enables the easy exchange of data between two or more metadata databases. For instance, if closely related information centres dealing with rural development, agricultural research, agricultural statistics, fisheries, agricultural universities, agricultural extension centres, etc., all use a common AP such as the AGRIS-AP, they will all be able to exchange information (at least at the level of common elements) with each other much more easily than if each of them follow their own metadata schemes.

An Application profile is defined as a type of metadata schema comprising data elements drawn from one or more namespaces, combined together by implementors, and optimised for a particular local application. This model allows different communities to use the DC elements for core descriptive information with extensions which make sense within a more limited area or discipline. The idea is to ensure many metadata databases to be able to exchange data with each other because all of them have the same core elements. In view of the fact that there are more than one internationally accepted metadata scheme in use, *e.g.*, MARC-21, DCMES, there are computer programmes which allow the transformation of data in one scheme to another. This allows the exchange of data at the base level

Inevitably, however, when data from one metadata schema is converted into another, there is bound to be loss of data. In today's globalised, networked world, the use of DC is widespread in many digital repositories and especially those subscribing to concepts of and the software compliant with the protocols of the Open Archives Initiative (OAI). Effective information networking today requires that libraries utilise software that supports newer metadata standards such as Dublin Core and become capable of contributing to and participate in such initiatives. As a result library automation solutions now need to provide support to interoperable standards such as DCMES Libraries in India seeking automation solutions need to take into account the need for software to support

MARKUP LANGUAGES

How should metadata be actually represented within a computer is another area which has received considerable attention. For instance in MARC-21, the metadata is represented using tags, indicators and subfield codes. The idea is that it should be possible for a computer programme to easily identify the title of a resource, its creator, kind of resource, etc.

The tagged structure was invented in the 1950's when on-line storage was expensive. In fact this structure was well suited for variable length records such as bibliographic records on magnetic tape. However, the emergence of the web and formats such as HTML which are Markup langauges and the fact that many computer applications, especially Internet browsers, can easily interpret data in such formats. The fact that on-line storage has become cheap thanks to hard disk technology, has made markup languages as the preferred way of representing data in computers. More recently the development of XML and its advantages over HTML have made XML as the *lingua franca* of data on the web. XML representation of data in a computer has following advantages:

- There is clear demarcation between content and display unlike with HTML
- Each application area (*e.g.*, banking, e-commerce, libraries, chemistry, geophysics, etc.,) can define Markup tags specific to their area. The XML tags and their definitions in each application area is agreed upon internationally (or as W3C standards) and these definitions are all provided as what is known as a Document Type Definition (DTD). The DTD is accessible at a web site and all XML documents in the area are validated against such DTDs to ensure consistency of data transmitted across the web.
- XML data is textual data and is therefore not subject to the quirks of proprietary software such as word processing. Thus XML data is readable by computer programmes irrespective of the operating system platform being used by a computer that connects to the data over the web. In a sense therefore XML data is future-proof.
- Due to the wide spread use of XML in web-based systems, there are standard open source computer programmes (freely downloadable from the web) that can handle (search, index) such data.
- Many library-related metadata standards such as MARC-21 and Dublin Core have already developed DTDs for the storage of data in XML form and for inter-conversion of data, *e.g.*, there is a DTD which allows MARC-21 data to be converted into MARC-XML form using a DTD that has been developed by the LOC and *vice versa*.

- Of special interest to libraries: XML's fixed character set is Unicode (and its extensions), which allows diacritics, special characters, and non-Roman data to be handled like ordinary text. HTML was heavily oriented to English and did inhibit its use in other languages.
- Due to Unicode and platform neutrality, XML offers the greatest promise of data longevity (or future proofing), as hardware, software, and network protocols continue to change.
- XML also provides for the unambiguous identification of complex data structures that can be treated as objects, well suited for bibliographic data.

Many of the new metadata standards such as Dublin Core and Application Profiles, expose their data as XML files due to the advantages of XML. The LoC also has made available a DTD to convert MARC records to XML. New ILMS are expected to provide the import of data in XML formats to local structures. As of today, the thinking is that it is not a question of choice between XML and MARC, or between XML and relational databases. The attempt will be to see how these technologies can be used synergistically to enable greater and seamless integration of library resources with the many other web resources. There is little doubt that effective library and information networking requires that libraries pay more and more attention to software that will allow them to use the new markup languages in their database and networking transactions.

INTEROPERABILITY STANDARDS

A simple definition of the term interoperability is the ability of software and hardware on different machines (and on different networks) from different vendors to share data. Interoperability may also be said to be an approach for dealing with the diversity and heterogeneity of the marketplace. Interoperability includes the exchange of data, records, and messages between computer systems across different hardware, operating systems, and networks. The greater the ease and seamlessness of the exchanges, the greater is the interoperability. Interoperability is sought to be achieved by establishing standards that different vendors of software and hardware can adopt so that they can share data and information. When two or more organisations exchange records on a regular basis, such as the transfer between shared cataloguing services and local systems, these arrangements are manageable.

Similarly, when libraries migrate from one library automation system to another, they can plan and implement a one-time data transfer. Today's requirements are much more complex, however. Ideally, libraries would like to treat multiple bibliographic databases as comprising an online, real-time, virtual digital library. Such a structure would enable libraries to exchange records on a casual, *ad hoc* basis, and would enable information seekers to search one or more external digital libraries as though all were one single resource. Only recently has it become possible to support generic clientserver relationships between information systems. The most advanced is the z39.50 standard that is being implemented for online catalogues and other bibliographic retrieval systems.

THE Z39.50 STANDARD

ANSI/NISO z39.50 is the American National Standard Information Retrieval Application Service Definition and Protocol Specification for Open Systems Interconnection. Version 3 of the standard with new facilities and services was released in 1995. ANSI/NISO z39.50 defines a standard procedure for two computers to communicate for the purpose of information retrieval. z39.50 makes it easier to use large information databases by standardising the procedures and features for searching and retrieving information.

Specifically, z39.50 supports information retrieval in a distributed, client and server environment, where a computer operating as a client submits a search request (*i.e.*, a query) to another computer acting as an information server. Software on the server performs a search on one or more databases and creates a result set of records that meet the criteria of the search request. The server returns records from the result set to the client for processing. The power of z39.50 lies in its ability to separate the user interface on the client side from the information servers, search engines, and databases. Z39.50 provides a consistent view of information from a wide variety of sources, and it offers client implementors the capability to integrate information from a range of databases and servers. ANSI/NISO z39.50 can be implemented on any platform. In other words z39.50 enables different computer systems—with different operating systems hardware, search engines, database management systems—to interoperate and work together *seamlessly*.

A z39.50 implementation enables one interface to access multiple systems, providing end users with nearly transparent access to other systems. Users access multiple systems with the familiar commands and displays of their own local systems, without having to learn new commands and search techniques. Such searches are called Federated Searches. The results of the searches are presented on the local system - again, in the formats and styles that users are accustomed to. Originally developed for use in computer communications networks using Open System Interconnection (OSI) protocols, z39.50 is now successfully operational in the environment of the Internet.

Interoperability testing of various z39.50 implementations has made it clear that the transport services (*i.e.*, the TCP/IP) of the Internet could be used successfully for the protocol. Using z39.50 over the Internet is a major step forward. Z39.50 implementations are available both as standalone applications as well as integral parts of an integrated library automation system (ILMS). In today's networked world, a library automation system that provides federated searching capabilities for its users will obviously be at a great advantage than others.

WEB SERVICES PROTOCOL-BASED APPLICATIONS FOR LIBRARY NETWORKING

Although the z39.50 protocol has been around since before the Internet era, there are several problems with this implementation of federated searching. Some of these are:

- Z39.50 is a complex and high-level protocol
- The implementation barrier is high for present web-based systems
- Federated search results from different servers are retrieved at various times depending on the availability of the server and network resources. In other words, this protocol is very information resource and band width sensitive.

As a result of these limitations, a new generation of services have been developed using web services protocols for federated searching. The two new services are SRW (Search and Retrieve Web Service) and SRU (Search and Retrieve URL Service). These new protocols have several advantages:

- All the advantages of Z39.50
- Implementation barrier is very low for web based systems, since this is based on high level web-based protocols
- SRW works with all high level protocols, *viz.*

SRW and SRU are web Services-based protocols for querying Internetaccessible databases and returning search results. SRW and SRU requests and results are similar, their difference lies in the ways the queries and results are encapsulated and transmitted between client and server applications. SRW uses existing, well tested and easily available technologies such as Simple Object Access Protocol (SOAP) and XPath in order to perform what has been done in the past using proprietary solutions. The design has had the benefit of 20 years of experience with the Z39.50 information retrieval protocol, and is both robust and easy to understand while still retaining the important aspects of its predecessor.

A SRW query is represented in CQL, the "Common Query Language", designed for human readable, human writeable, intuitive queries. It supports very simple queries — for example an unqualified single term (*e.g.*, "cat") — but maintains the expressiveness of more complex languages, to represent arbitrarily complex queries. Many libraries in the west using specialised software and/or a new generation ILMS have begun implementing SRU/SRW protocols. Similarly, many libraries have also made their databases accessible via SRW/SRU servers. Indian libraries must become aware of these developments as they will undoubtedly increase a library's capability to provide easier access to specialised databases in single or federated mode. Provision of such access is a clear way of differentiating libraries from their competitors.

OPENURL

More and more full text resources are now becoming accessible on web sites of publishers, libraries, professional bodies. These resources are identified by a URL. However, when the web site decides to move the resource to some other location within the site or even remove it from their site, the old URL captured in a database will no longer point to the resource. This leads to frustration for the user. This is particularly so when users search journal article databases or when they access e-journals. Access to the full text of articles is sought and this is where the concept of a persistent URL becomes necessary.

However, users, working as they do in an organisational context, have defined access and view privileges for e-serials and databases. For instance, the organisation they work for may not have access to an e-journal's full text but only to the abstract of articles. The OpenURL standard is a protocol for interoperability between an information resource, *e.g.*, an on-line or CD-ROM database and a service component, referred to as a link server, which offers localised services. The underlying concept of the OpenURL standard is that links should lead a user to appropriate resources. A link server, such as the SFX server from the ILMS, ExLibris, defines the context of the user.

When the link server accepts an OpenURL as input, it acts on it to provide users with services that comply with their institution's collections and policies. The OpenURL standard enables a user who has retrieved an article citation, for example, to obtain immediate access to the "most appropriate" copy of that object through the implementation of extended linking services (also called context-sensitive linking). The selection of the best copy is based on user and organisational preferences regarding the location of the copy, its cost, and agreements with information suppliers, and similar considerations. The link from the source citation to a "resolver" (the link server), which stores the preference information and the links to the appropriate material.

A *link resolver* interprets incoming OpenURLs, takes the local holdings and access privileges of that institution (usually a library) into account, and displays links to appropriate resources. A link resolver allows the library to provide a range of library-configured links and services, including links to the full-text, a local catalogue to check print holdings, document delivery or ILL services, databases, search engines, etc. Many of today's information providers can generate and output OpenURLs. Libraries that have access to an OpenURL compliant link server such as SFX, must furnish an OpenURL for their full text resources, *e.g.*, their own monographs, reports, etc., in digital form.

The OpenURL system works in conjunction with a body called CrossRef, an independent membership association, founded and directed by publishers. CrossRef's mandate is to connect users to primary research content, by enabling publishers to do collectively what they cannot do individually. CrossRef establishes Digital Object Identifiers (DOI), an identifier using an open standard, to scholarly and professional publications. CrossRef operates a cross-publisher citation linking system that allows a researcher to click on a reference citation on one publisher's platform and link directly to the cited content on another publisher's platform, subject to the target publisher's access control practices. The citation-linking network today covers millions of articles and other content items from several hundred scholarly and professional publishers.

CrossRef DOIs link to publisher response pages, which include the full bibliographic citation and abstract, as well as full-text access (for authenticated users or at no charge, as determined by the publisher). The publisher response page often includes other linking options, such as pay-per-view access, journal table of contents and homepage, and associated resources. CrossRef is a collaborative membership network, and not a product for purchase. DOI, an open standard, is an alphanumeric identifier for digital content, such as a book or journal article.

The DOI is paired with the object's electronic address, or URL, in an updateable central directory, and is published in place of the URL in order to avoid broken links while allowing the content to move as needed. DOIs are distributed by publishers and by CrossRef, and there is no end-user charge associated with their use. As an identifier, the DOI can be incorporated into many different systems and databases. The DOI system provides a framework for persistent identification, managing intellectual content, managing metadata, and linking customers with content suppliers. The key benefits of the CrossRef DOI for libraries are:

- Truly persistent links
- Increased usage of acquired resources
- Expanded access to content not owned
- Enhanced and customisable localised linking
- Metadata retrieval privileges at no cost to most libraries

Although these new fangled standards seem complex at first glance, it is important that Indian libraries become familiar with these and look for solutions which will support these new standards. The move towards provision of access to full text, the fact that more and more digital resources are on the web, the emergence of the open archives initiatives (OAI) and digital repositories has made it absolutely vital that libraries embrace these new standards and technologies if they wish to differentiate themselves from their competitors.

OPEN ACCESS INITIATIVE—PROTOCOL FOR METADATA HARVESTING

The OAI-Protocol for Metadata Harvesting (OAI-PMH) defines a mechanism for harvesting records containing metadata from digital repositories. The OAI-PMH gives a simple technical option for data providers to make their metadata available to service providers, based on the open standards HTTP and XML. The metadata that is harvested may be in any format that is agreed by a community, although unqualified Dublin Core is specified to provide a basic level of interoperability. Thus, metadata from many sources can be gathered together in one database, and services can be provided based on this centrally harvested, or "aggregated" data.

The link between this metadata and the related content is not defined by the OAI protocol. OAI-PMH does not provide a search across this data, it simply makes it possible to bring the data together in one place. In order to provide services, the harvesting approach must be combined with other service mechanisms, *e.g.*, a search, alerting services. Two players in the Open Access movement are Data Providers and Service Providers.

A Data Provider maintains one or more repositories (web servers) that support the OAI-PMH as a means of exposing metadata. A Service Provider, on the other hand, issues OAI-PMH requests to data providers and uses the metadata as a basis for building value-added services. A Service Provider in this manner is "harvesting" the metadata exposed by Data Providers.

They use the harvested metadata for the purpose of providing one or more services across all the data. The types of services that may be offered include a search interface, peer-review system, etc. One organisation can play both roles, offering both data for harvesting and end-user services. Libraries now have the possibility to selectively harvest useful metadata from one or more OAI-PMH compliant archives and into their own database and provide search and access not only to metadata but also to digital content for the benefit of their users.. Similarly, library's can also become data providers and allow other libraries and information centres to harvest metadata for their users. OAI-PMH is a simple protocol based on HTTP and XML, it allows for rapid deployment. The figure below is a graphical representation of the way OAI-PMH works.

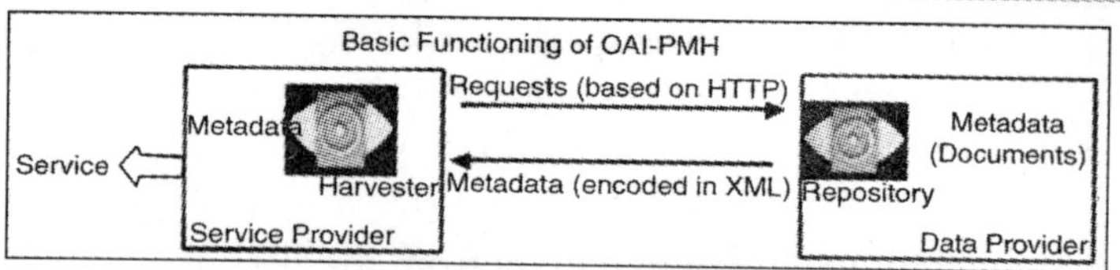

Fig 3.1 Basic Functioning of OAI-PMH

CONCLUSION

Infrastructure may be likened to the foundation of a building and standards to the bricks. Only when these two are cemented by appropriate software that useful applications can result. Libraries and information centres in India have always been faced with difficulties when it comes to choosing software to automate their libraries. This problem is even more exacerbated today when they are facing competition from other players as they will need to justify the choice of a software even more convincingly to their managements than before.

In such a scenario, the best approach is to concentrate not so much on criteria that will help the library to become more efficient but on how software will make it possible for the library to utilise networked resources for the benefit of their users. In doing so, libraries would do well to ensure that the software they choose will support networking and exploitation of web resources apart from automating their internal operations.

In other words, the software that they choose must support international data and open interoperability standards, and should be web-based because only such software will be flexible, have the possibility of the integrating the access to the library's resources along with other web resources that users have become accustomed to. Some of the criteria in choosing appropriate software are given below.

- Does the software support international data standards such as MARC-21 and the DCMES?
- Does the software support copy cataloguing using authoritative MARC-21 cataloguing sources via the web?

- Will the software allow the library to create its own network of libraries cost-effectively? Will it be possible to use the web to allow networked libraries to utilise a single server/software infrastructure? This will be costeffective and will expand access to resources for the users.
- Will the software allow federated searching of one or more library and specialised subject databases using an interoperability standard such as z39.50 or newer ones such as SRU/SRW? This will allow access to useful resources beyond that of the library.
- Will the software allow the building of an OAI-PMH compliant institutional repository of self-archived materials and will it allow the library to harvest metadata from other OAI-PMH compliant repositories? This will allow specialised resources (journal articles, reports) and full text to become accessible via the library's interface.
- Will the software allow the entry, storage and searching of data in non-Roman scripts? This is particularly important for Indian academic libraries which deal with materials in one or more Indian languages in their collections.
- Will the software allow other libraries to download metadata into their databases?
- Will the software allow access to digital content such as full text, images, audio, video, web pages, and databases and full text on CD-ROMs (that may be mounted on an institution's CD Server).
- Does the software allow the description of a wide range of materials including analytics, web resources, learning objects, audio, video, etc., and not only conventional monograph and serial items?
- Does the software's OPAC allow flexible searching of library holdings and does it empower users by offering access to other services, *e.g.*, interlibrary loans, document delivery services, alerting services and access to other web resources, e-serials, search engines?

4

Networking

A network is a social structure made of nodes which are generally individuals or organisations. It indicates the ways in which they are connected through various social familiarities ranging from casual acquaintance to close familial bonds. Networking is basically an inter institutional arrangement intended to break information isolation. The term was first coined by Barnes. Networking involves a set of skills and activities relying heavily on effective interpersonal communication for gathering, processing, and moving information in organisation.

Networking is a set of behaviours that take place within the context of organisations. However, networking has become a popular term in the day to day conversation and is often considered to be related to job seeking and personal advancement with an emphasis on self-promotion and trying to use others for ones' own ends. None of us can survive in business or other profession without a strong network of information and referral sources. Every person has a network of old schoolmates, relatives, colleagues from former jobs or leisure activities, and friends.

The critical factor is your mindset towards networking–recognising networking as important, not a waste of time. Networking is valuable not simply because of the information you gather, but because of the sense of cooperation or goodwill that you create.

Networking is often considered as the hidden side of organisational leadership. The human network is the social structure composed of individuals, friends, collaborators or other organisations connected through technology using a variety of devices - personal computers, mobile phones, gaming consoles and PDAs. In many instances the term is described synonymously with the architecture of participation. It is the intersection of communications networks and social networks - a telecommunications network where people are the endpoints.

DEFINITION AND CONCEPT OF NETWORKING

Networking is the building and maintaining of relationships with a wide range of individuals, groups, or institutions who share common interests, goals, or expertise. Networking implies that the relationships between people are the determining factor in programmes. Women face different challenges than men in the workplace. To meet these challenges successfully women need to network. Networking is about sharing information, ideas, resources, opportunities. Members of a network look to each other for advice, tips on jobs, careers and employment and create a support system for each other.

These informal strategic alliances can benefit you greatly. Networking is emerging as an important concept in the study of professional effectiveness and advancement, leadership, and organisations. It has been linked to studies of leadership power and influence skills, careerdevelopment and promotion tactics, organisational structure and communication processes. Networking has become popularised and is often considered to be related to job seeking and personal advancement, with an emphasis on self-promotion and trying to use others for one's own ends.

NEED FOR NETWORKING

In any organisation there are structured groups like different departments, or work groups and unstructured or informal groups. Individuals' involvement in unstructured groups is important, because networking is becoming the best way to accomplish things in organisation. Researchers have found that workers discussed new and innovative ideas in an unstructured group more freely than in a structured group or in a hierarchical role relationship.

VARIOUS FEATURES OF NETWORKING

Networking is characterised by the following features:

- Ongoing, purposeful interaction
- Cooperation
- Relationships
- People centeredness
- Complex and diverse interconnections
- Open ended and flexible progression

NETWORKING COMPONENTS

It is essential to approach networking systematically. In order to develop a good network you should be able to answer the following types of questions:

- In which organisations/ events do you need to be visible?
- What kinds of referral sources do you need, and where/ how can you meet them?
- Who can influence potential people to choose you, and how can you meet them?
- Who are already your advocates and can introduce you to others?

Different people have different attitudes to networking. All persons are not natural net workers. Some can develop strong networking skills with a little help, and others are really not comfortable meeting strangers especially in new cultures. You would find different attitudes towards networking among different types of net worker as you can make out below.

- *The passive net worker:* They have little interest in meeting new people. Instead, they will gravitate to people they already know, wasting the chance to expand their contacts.
- *The inquisitive net worker:* This type of people takes initiative but behaves like a detective interrogating suspects. They draw out other people and may learn

a lot, but sooner of later the fact that they do not share any information will make others stop trusting them.

- *Social networker:* This type takes appropriate initiative in meeting new people but keeps the conversation on a social level. They may be very popular and receive many social invitations – and so can be very valuable in your networking strategy. However, they need to understand how to engage in commercial information exchanges as well.
- *Dedicated networker:* They initiate appropriately and are constantly looking for ways to be helpful to others. In return, the latter often share with them valuable market information and intelligence. These staff members are the heart of your networking team and should receive your active support and are rewarded for their efforts.

Even some of those who have strongly supported the view that effectiveness of networking centres around, the objective to further ones' own interest have started seeing the limited scope of this self serving framework. They say that knowing how to network is practivally knowing how to be helpful to the people with whom we work and ask for help in return. In reality, interdependence not independence is the key to getting somewhere in the work world. Such attitude expresses what is best about networking ability to create an effective support system for yourself that also works to the advantage of others. Networking is now becoming as emerging style of functioning within the organisation. People are increasingly learning from one another horizontally; everyone is becoming a resource for everyone else; and each person is receiving professional support and assistance from many directions. In this scenario, one can identify the following as strategies for successful networking

- Finding the right track to multiple sources of information related to a project;
- Bridging the information flow between functions such as finance and marketing;

- Communicating by both formal and informal means to accomplish projects;
- Doing things and/or gathering information without overpowering others;
- Managing the give and take of information flow within an organisation or between organisations, often outside formal organisation lines and;
- Facilitating the interchange among individuals who serve as resources to obtain a specific goal.

It has been found that networking can be a decisive factor in the woking of a successful organisation. Research has proved that workers are more likely to talk about new ideas with those colleagues with whom they also discussed work and personal matters. Tacit knowledge is shared relatively easily between individuals within the community, often without ever being made explicit. And those who are well integrated into networks of social relationship at work are more likely to participate in decision-making. They can see clearly how they contribute to group performance and share in the rewards of group performance. It has also been found that highest number of innovation has taken place in those organisations where collaboration, free flow of information and coalitions built of supporters are the dominant characteristics.

NETWORKING THROUGH INFORMATION AND COMMUNICATION TECHNOLOGY (ICT)

Nowadays, organisations are investing in ICT that create intra-organisational electronic network. The purpose is to have "bridging ties" between geographically dispersed organisational members. The main objective is to provide a platform to communication through which individuals working on similar problems may quickly ask each other for help on task related problem. Educators and policy makers need to stay alert to the need for programmes that maintain the principle of providing a positive, useful, and quality service.

- *Professional development:* New Technologies, while helpful in certain key ways, also create new problems, the foremost of which is training individuals (learners and teachers) how to implement them in a cost-effective manner. Sometimes the training process becomes very expensive, and nearly counterproductive (when in the midst of repaid platform and software changes). The Internet promises, in some respects to be relatively easy to train on and with.

- *Technological lifelong learning:* Using Online networking technology and the Internet not only provides adult learners with new opportunities for literacy and basic skills instruction but the use of these technologies themselves provide new technological literacy skills that adult learners can utilise in the work place, for personal reasons, and in the future for additional lifelong learning at higher levels.

In sum, Internet-based network technology is one of the most promising areas for literacy work in the world. The benefits of this technology seem well matched with the following problems in the literacy field:

- The dispersed and diverse population of adult learners,
- The limited and thinly distributed expertise in learning diagnosis, and
- The need to connect learners and instructions interactively in an asynchronous manner that takes advantages of learners needs for independence along with their unavailability for formal classroom instruction.

The uses of technology for adult literacy and adult education have been growing exponentially in recent years, from computer-assisted instruction to the information highway and to the simple improvements engendered by the use of personal computers in management and information systems.

TECHNOLOGY, THE INTERNET AND ADULT LITERACY

One can argue that in theory, electronicbased technologies are a source of exponential growth in the field of adult literacy. All things being equal, that is, inexpensive access to broadband width of internet facility, uninterrupted supply of power and clear link between literacy and poverty alleviation, it is possible to effectively work on the interface between technology, the Internet and adult literacy.

Electronic Technologies

Computers, wireless communications, videotapes, and the like are now being incorporated into elementary, secondary, business, and college level education. Adult literacy programmes, in contrast, still lag far behind in using these newer technologies for instruction. Studies show that many adult literacy programmes have a foothold in technology, but this is mainly in the use of microcomputers for administrative purposes, not instructional ones. Economic considerations clearly are a major impediment to technology implementation in adult literacy programmes.

Need of Network in Adult Literacy

These technologies hold enormous promise for the future because they can:

- Reduce the isolation that many adult literacy providers and students experience,
- Facilitate communication among staff and students within and between programmes
- Increase access to high quality materials and emerging research,
- Streamline administrative and reporting processes, and
- Help to provide the delivery vehicle for innovative instructional and staff development approaches.

However, we need to keep in mind that across these new technologies, there is also inadequate staff training and lack of information on effective implementation and specialised uses.

ADVANTAGES OF NETWORKING AND INTERNET TECHNOLOGY

There are some clear advantages of networking and Internet technology both for adult learners and for adult literacy programmes.

For learners, this would include:

- Reaching learners outside of the classroom,
- Using learning time more efficiently,
- Sustaining motivation
- Individualising instruction and
- Providing access to information tools.

For adult literacy programmes, this would include:

- Improved recruiting and training of learners,
- Improving curriculum
- Meeting staff development needs
- Enhancing assessment and curriculum, and
- Streamlining coordination, management and administration.

INTERNET SERVICES

The Internet allows each of us to share information and resources such as government documents, electronic publications, online books, media publishing, human anatomical images, computer software, bibliographic and full-text databases, speeches, live concerts, animal sounds, and motion videos. The Internet's dynamic nature is delivered from world citizens contributing their time, resources and energies to each other. Users consult electronic resources at libraries; download computer shareware and software upgrades. A few usages of the Internet can be listed.

- To trade with people or other organisations
- To access information on Internet, you need a browser-software. Examples of the browser can be Netscape, Internet Explorer etc.

The World Wide Web (WWW) can be defined as a hypertext, multimedia, distributed information system that provides links to hypertext documents, as well as too many other Internet tools and databases. There are several features that are unique to the Web that make it the most advanced information system to appear on the Internet to date.

Network-based Information Services:

- Resource Sharing, Virtual Libraries, Computer Mediated Communication, Web Publishing, Other Services

- Infrastructure Requirements Hardware, Software, Human ware, Technologies for Networking, Network architecture etc
- Organisation of Information Resources Digital resources, Non-print media, Content creation, Metadata tools, Research networks, Institution networks etc
- Network Policy and Governance Participation in INFLIBNET, Legal and Copyright issues, Economics of centralised database services Institutional policies etc.

ELECTRONIC NETWORKS OF PRACTICE (EnoPS)

In an effort to replicate traditional social networks electronically, organisations are now investing in computer-mediated communication technologies to facilitate knowledge sharing regardless of time and space constraints. These emergent virtual communities are referred as electronic networks of practice (EnoPs). Needles to say, communication within this network of practice occurs primarily through computer-based communication technologies suh as bulletin board, listservs etc. One of the main characteristics of ENoPs is that the participants in the network interact with one another to help each other solve problems.

By posting a message, individuals seeking help can reach out others who can provide valuable knowledge and insight in response. The posting of messaes and responses is recorded like a conversation beteen participants. This shows active mutual engagement in problem solving; and the characteristic of mutual engagement distinguishes it from more static form of electronic knowledge exchange, such as document repositories and other types of database. Another characteristic of an ENoP is the fact that the technology supports any number of participants.

As a result knowledge seekers are not limited to asking only experts whom they personally know or able to identify, thus increasing the possibility of connecting with someone willing and able to help. In addition, knowledge in an ENoP is typically archived and available to all participants in the network. This ultimately creates and online repository of questions and answers that can be referred to later by any individual regardless of the fact whether he or she had participated in the original discussion. The value of an ENoP increases dramatically as the number of participants rises. Moreover, in an ENoP, participation is open to anyone with a desire to interact.

The electronic links created by the Internet and related technologies that enable individuals to communicate are practically ubiquitous, thus membership is open to anyone with a desire whether they want to participate as well as how often they participate. They have the choice to determine what they want to contribute, choosing what knowledge they are willing to disclose as well as the length of the message they contribute influencing the quality and helpfulness of the knowledge exchanged.

The characteristic of discretionary choices regarding participation and knowledge sharing differntiates an ENoP from other form of virtual work, such as virtual teams in which the members of participants are expected to coordinate effects to deliver a specific outcome. In addition to these, participants in an ENoP are strangers. Knowledge exchange is an ENoP occurs between people regardless of personal acquaintance, familiarity or location. Since participation is voluntary, knowledge seekers have no control over who responds to their questions. On the contrary, in a traditional social network, people typically know one another and interact overtime creating expectations of obligations and reciprocity that are enforced through social sanctions.

NEED OF NETWORKING

Electronic Networks of Practice is an excellent means of improving one's own level of technical competence. Additionally it helps to keep current with technical developments as well as to know who was actively working in different areas. Technically or otherwise people gain competitiveness. There seem to be a variety of reasons why people help each other. As the saying goes, nothing comes free, in order to receive help from the network, individuals feel obligated to help others in return, a strong sense of reciprocity. In some organisations, like knowledge management companies, helping others is a part of their job.

Through their participation they are able to improve level of technical competence of network as a whole and ultimately enhance organisation's competitiveness in the market. The participants of EnoP gain exposure to critical new ideas. They get help and advice not available locally. Studies indicate that individuals participate in EnoPs outperform their colleagues who primarily rely on their colleagues for knowledge and advice. A database of all the postings/ questions can be made. This shall help individuals to find topics as well as a means to educate people on how to use e-mail or list serve technology give here examples of Adult education/ community participation questions.

PROBLEMS ASSOCIATED WITH NETWORKING

In case of List serve mailing lists, even though mail is received in the mail box, yet there is much unsolicited mail. The receiver has to go through that. It wastes his much time which otherwise could be utilised in some productive work. In a discussion form, the participants are required to enter forum actively otherwise he/she gets no postings of the network. An online CoP may be ephemeral and the knowledge created may be lost, unless proper infrastructure is in place that can sustain what may be learned.

EnoP AND PARTICIPATION AND HELPING OTHERS

Higher levels of participation and tenure in the EnoP are associated with both acquisition of knowledge from participation in the network and contributing knowledge to others. In addition, both knowledge acquisition from and knowledge contribution to the network are positively related to individual performance. Level of participation in the network is more important for supporting positive knowledge outcomes than the length of time an individual has participated. This implies that newcomers to the network can reap the same benefits of participation as long as standing participants. EnoPs are a type of collective in which the knowledge exchanged and created is the collective's public good. Mutual engagement in an EnoP is open and voluntary. Participation typically results in the creation of a knowledge repository of archived messages that is available to all individuals regardless of their original participation.

KNOWLEDGE SHARING AND ELECTRONIC NETWORKS

Tacit knowledge is shared relatively easily between individuals within the community, often without ever being made explicit. Furthermore, these tightly knit social structures facilitate the creation of a shared identify through the development of a common language and social capital (such as norms of behaviour, trust, and obligation), resulting in strong social ties between individuals. These characteristics have been argued as essential for the continuous incremental improvements in the community's practice and the reason why CoPs are centres for learning and innovation within organisations. In contrast, interactions in an EnoP are limited text based, asynchronous, computermediated communication. As a result, the ability of members to develop a shared identity and common language through narration, collaboration and social construction is hampered. However, EnoPs have a greater reach than CoPs and support the creation of weak electronic "bridging ties" between unlimited numbers of like minded others from across the globe. Due to the extensive reach of these networks, individuals benefit from EnoPs since they gain access to new information, expertise, and ideas that are often not available locally.

COMPUTER NETWORKS

NETWORKING THROUGH COMPUTERS

A computer is emerging and no one could keep himself/ herself away from it any longer. But, what are the types of a network within the arena of computers? Those are LAN, MAN and WAN. Not only this, there are certain topologies associated with it and there are certain components which carry out these functions. We need to acquaint ourselves with these technical words and their usages when we move to the area of networking through computers and extend its use in reaching out to adult learners.

Types of Network

Based on geographical dispersion of computers there are mainly three types of network.

1. Local Area Network (LAN)
2. Metropolitan Area Network (MAN)
3. Wide Area Network (WAN)

Local Area Network (LAN)

In this type of network computers and other communication devices are in a small area and are connected together (networked). The area can be single building, cluster of buildings in the same campus. Examples can be Local Area Network of Lab in which you may be working or a library which you may be using.

Metropolitan Area Network (MAN)

A Metropolitan Area Network is basically a bigger version of LAN and normally uses similar technology. It might cover a group of nearby corporate offices or it can be in a city. It can be private or public.

Wide Area Network (WAN)

Computers can be farther apart like covering cities, countries or even continents. The computers are connected by telephone lines or radio waves or optical fibres.

Network Topologies (NT)

Topology refers to the shape of a network or network's layout. How different nodes in a network are connected to each other and how they communicate is determined by the network's topology. There are four most common network topologies, namely,

- Bus Topology,

- Star Topology,
- Ring Topology and
- Mesh Topology.

Star Topology

All devices are connected to a central hub. Nodes communicate across the network by passing data through the hub.

Bus Topology

All devices are connected to a central cable, called the bus or backbone.

Ring Topology

All devices are connected to one another in the shape of a closed loop, so that each device is connected directly to two other devices, one on either side of it.

Mesh Topology or Point to Point Network

Devices are connected with many redundant inter-connections between network nodes. In a true mesh topology every node has a connection to every other node in the network.

Network Components

The following are essential components for computer networking.

- Network hardware
- Transmission media and
- Network software

Network Hardware

The basic component of computer network hardware is a computer. Computers on a network can be divided into two categories,

1. Server and
2. Clients or nodes.

Server is the computer of higher power, and speed. It costs more. To this computer resources are attached. And the clients, also known as nodes access, are the resources which are attached to server. In peer to peer computer networks there are no servers.

Transmission Media

Communication of data propagation and processing of signals is called transmission. Signals travel from transmitter to receiver via a path. This path is called medium. Medium can be guided or unguided.

Guided Media

In guided media, data is sent along a physical path, *i.e.,* cables. There are several types of cables used in network. The type of cable chosen for a network is related to the network's topology, protocol and size. Different types of cables:

- Coaxial cable looks like cable that brings the cable TV signal to television.
- Twisted pair copper wire cable looks like phone cable. Twisted pair cables come in two varieties, a. shielded and b. unshielded.
- Optical fibre cable

Unguided Media

Here no wire is installed. The data communication is predominantly sent by radio waves and microwaves.

Network Card

As suggested, discuss about networking software. But hardware has also to be connected. Most important part of connection is the network card. This is the middle part of connection. These cards are 8 bit cards, 16 bit cards and 32 bit cards. Each card has its own method of sending information (network protocol) through the cable. The most commonly used is Ethernet Protocol. A network card is called Interface card, network adapter, a NIC etc. It is a circuit board or chip which allows the computer to communicate to other computers on a network.

Modem (MODulator/ DEModulator)

A modem converts digital signals (computer signals) from the computer into analogue signals for transmission and vice versa for reception over a telephone line. There are four basic types of modems for a PC:

1. External,
2. USB,
3. Internal and
4. Built-in.

External and USB are set on your desk outside the PC, while as Internal and Built-in are inside the PC. Present day modems have 56 kilobites per second speed. ISDN (Integrated Services Digital Network) circuits are digital. In this conversion from digital to analogue is not required.

Switch

Switches are basically bridges, but usually have multiple ports. Switches connect network segments, using a table of addresses to determine the segment on which a packet needs to be transmitted.

Hubs

A hub is used to connect multiple computers and devices via a dedicated cable. It is cheap and connections are easy. It generally has 4, 8, 12, 24 ports.

Router

These are used to connect networks and to determine the optimal path along which the network traffic should be forwarded. They are occasionally called gateways. There are other network devices like repeaters, bridges, ports, etc.

Network Operating Software

Network operating software (NOS) is a collection of software and associated protocols that allow a set of autonomous computers, which are interconnected by a computer network, to be used together in a convenient and costeffective manner. It is similar to any other operating system like windows, DOS, etc. except it operates over more than one computer. It controls operation of the network system, including who uses it, when they can use it, what they have access to, and which network resources are available. At a basic level, the NOS allows network users to share files and peripherals such as disks and printers. They provide data integrity and security. The examples can be categories of NOS: The NetWare, LAN Manager, Solaris and Windows 2000 etc. The main categories of network software are:

- Peer to peer software and
- Client/ Server-based.

Peer to Peer Software

In peer to peer networking operating software users can share resources and files located on their computers and can access shared resources on other computers. There is no central server. All computers in the network are equal. They have similar capabilities and resources. Examples of Peer to peer network software are Windows XP, Windows 98. When you are working in Microsoft Office Word under Windows environment, you can share the shared documents. It is possible because Windows XP is peer to peer networking software.

Client Server Based (Two Tier)

This software is in two parts. One part which includes functions and services resides in one or more exclusive (dedicated) computers. This part is called server. It provides security and access to resources. Another part called 'client' resides on other computers (nodes/ client). They access resources on the server. The network operating system allows multiple users to simultaneously share the same resources irrespective of physical location. Examples of Server based networking software are: Novel Netware, Windows NT, UNIX, Window 2000 etc.

Client Server Based (Three Tier)

Here a client-software is split into two parts:

1. Browser (user-interface) (thin client) and
2. Logic.

Thus two tier client-server becomes three tier architecture. The logic which describes how to access and process data is moved to a new server. This new server is server for thin client. Nothing changes in the server side.

INTERNET

The Internet is a network of networks. It connects millions of computers and thousands of computer networks throughout the world. The Internet has revolutionised our society, our economy and our technological systems. The Internet represents one of the most successful examples of the benefits of sustained investment and commitment to research and development of the information infrastructure.

The Internet Society (ISOC) defines the Internet as a "global network of networks" which enables computers of all kinds to directly and transparently communicate and share services throughout the world. It provides for both communications capabilities and information services. It also constitutes a shared global resource of information, knowledge and means of collaboration and cooperation among countless diverse communities. For communication on Internet it uses standard protocol which is called transmission control protocol, Internet Protocol or TCP/IP. Standardised communication protocols allow similar, dissimilar, near and distant computers to communicate with one another. The Internet protocols and standards are being defined from time to time by various international organisation and committees after rigourous testing and reviewing.

Trends

You may like to know about Internet 2 and Internet 3, which reflect future rends in computer networks.

Internet 2

It is a consortium being led by 200 universities working in partnership with industry and government to develop and deploy advanced network applications and technologies, accelerating the creation of tomorrow's Internet.

Internet 3

It includes the US Government's initiative to provide high andwidth network service.

Adult Education

There are discussion groups and e-mail lists relating to adult learning. You may try to access some of the following resources.

Discussion Groups

- Alt.education.distance is a group that focuses on learning over the Internet, a form of distance education.
- Bit.listserv.edtech is an adult education discussion group.
- Misc.eeducation.adult is an adult education discussion group.

E-mail Lists

- ADNET is the adult education network
- URL: listserv@alpha.acast.nova.edu
- DEOS-L is the international forum for distance learning.
- URL: listserv@psuvm.psu.edu
- DISTED is an online chronicle of Distance Education and Communication
- URL: listserv@alpha.acast.nova.edu

Importance of Internet

The Internet is an "enabling technology". When its introduction is sensitive to local values and committed to local capacitybuilding, it offers important opportunities to

- *Open dialogue:* Low cost networking facilitates knowledge sharing, awareness of alternative perspectives, more open exchange
- *Improve governance:* Raising efficiency, transparency, participatory systems
- *Improve social and human rights conditions:* Expands access to better quality education, health care, disaster relief capacity and other services
- *Reduce poverty:* Opens new opportunities for bypassed groups (women, the poor, rural populations, children)

- *Introduce economic opportunities:* E-commerce, ICT-sector development etc.
- *Improve environmental management, GIS:* Food security early warning systems.
- *Support indigenous knowledge:* Communities document their knowledge.

Benefits of Internet

It supports and encourages the new learning environment, which is based on principles of active learning-reflecting the change in the culture of education from teacher-centred to learnercentred. The Internet can be used for a variety of purposes from a library. Some of the purposes are:

- To exchange e-mail instantly with institutions in India or abroad
- To participate in teleconferences with people on topics of internet or research problems like adult education
- To find out educational information from universities libraries and book stores all over the world
- To search on-line library catalogues for bibliographic data and other databases for textual data
- To have access to electronic journals, newsletters and in-house information of many organisations and institutions.

Disadvantages of Internet

Advances in communication media (VoIP, Instant messaging, e-mail), based on Internet technology have made computer mediated communication more rich and cheap. Yet, today, this potential for knowledge sharing is not fully realised. Indeed, the internet is by nature an anonymous medium in which people find it hard to place their trust. As a result, people who have had few or no face-to-face meetings are not likely to share knowledge.

ALTIN

The purpose of the Adult Literacy Technology Innovation

Network (ALTIN) technology training programme, begun in the mid-1990 was to provide basic instructional technology staff development for adult literacy teachers, including the basics of instructional technology and electronic online communications in a useful and userfriendly way, while at the same time building a network of practitioners who can, after the six months of training, assist other literacy programmes and practitioners by means of a mentoring process.

ALTIN has shown that an electronic training network works best when participants have established a human network among themselves when they are able to identify commonalities of interest and need, have established a level of trust and commitment among themselves, and can identify areas of collaboration and communication that will result in mutual benefit. Face-toface meetings appear to make such a people-to-people connection easier, helping to increase the level of trust, facilitating the identification of areas of mutual interest and concern among participants, and increasing the accountability and commitment that participants have to each other online.

SHELCOM: Focus on Learners

The shelter communications Literacy Network was an experimental Internetbased computer writing project for adults living in homeless shelters in Philadelphia, USA. The project began in 1993 and completed in 1995. These poorly educated adults also suffered from a variety of problems associated with drug and alcohol use. SHELCOM showed that such disadvantaged populations can be reached effectively through the Internet, in spite of the initial low literacy abilities of many participants.

Literacy Link

Distance education for learners and teachers: Literacy Link, funded by the U.S. Department of Education is designed to serve the large numbers of Americans who require additional basic skills instruction. As an Internet-based lifelong learning system, Literacy Link has two major goals:

1. To increase the access of adults to learning

opportunities that will enable them to obtain their high school diplomas, and

2. To improve the quality of instruction available to individuals and adult literacy providers nationwide through enhanced resources and expanded staff development.

Literacy Link is one of the first and most comprehensive initiatives to harness the power of the Internet to provide instruction and demand to adult learners, as well as communities, libraries, schools and homes.

Conclusions and Future Directions

The case studies illustrate a few of the opportunities that have become available through Internet. Some of them are staff development, reaching out to the disadvantaged, and taking advantage of the convenience of learning in the home or community. In the ALTIN case study, it was found that human networks are an essential component to the electronic networks that are now easily and cheaply available on the Internet. The SHELCOM project demonstrated that new technologies can be implemented with even the most difficult to reach and difficult-to-retain populations, using fairly simple networking and word-processing techniques. Literacy Link deals with how distance education can provide a cost-effective and comprehensive selflearning system for adult education in the home and community.

Information Production and Dissemination through Network

Production of information and its dissemination through network can be most effective if it comprises local content. As suggested, discuss here importance of local content and creation of local content in India. Then as suggested, look at creation of information that is demanddriven. There will be short pieces of information on creation of rural knowledge repositories and local web sites, databases, bulletin boards and e-mail lists.

Importance of Local Content

An education centre can provide people in the community

with access to computers to send and receive information. Centre should translate the need to provide people with access to content that they can use in their daily lives. Persons may need such practical content as adult literacy programmes, information on public benefits, information on health, consumer and credit information, and information related to employment and training. If a woman in the village has access to the Internet, she will not necessarily be able to use the information to improve her child's health because trying to get information from the Internet is like drinking from a fire hose – you don't know the source of the water.

Local content is a big challenge for an adult education centre. A multi-nation study by the International Institute for Communication and Development or IICD suggests that "easier access to globalised knowledge is fast turning us into 'consumers' of distant and potentially irrelevant information". Local content, the report says faces intense competition because big content initiatives by other groups tend to push their external content onto local communities. In the same vein, another IICD report suggests developing countries are being invaded by foreign ideas and values that may undermine or overwhelm local cultures.

Generation of Local Content in India

Here is a case study of a village knowledge centre. It shows how staff dealt with the issues of local, relevance and language. The centres, established in Pondicherry on the southeast coast of India by the M.S. Swaminathan Research Foundation (MSSRF), demonstrated ingenuity, creativity and sensitivity in developing their information products. In one case, coastal villages were highly dependent on weather and tides information.

Many fishermen were not literate. Village Knowledge Centre downloaded whether reports from digital network information and converted that to audio. The audio versions were then played on loudspeakers in the open air. In addition, project volunteers in the villages built their own information resources in the center to complement the external databases thereby providing local and localised information on agricultural, health and government programmes for low-income people, for example, a directory of general and crop insurance schemes; a list of about 130 schemes available as entitlements to rural families; a directory of hospitals and medical practitioners in Pondicherry – grouped according to their specialisations; bus and train schedules covering Pondicherry and two nearby towns; and pest management information for the sugarcane crop.

The content in the cases is based on Dagron and Harris. Information must be locally relevant and respond to the information needs of the potential users. In such ways these services shall contribute to social and economic community development and to sustainability of the adult education setup.

Demand Driven Information Production in the Warna Wired Village Project

The project area is a cluster of 70 villages in the Sangli district of Maharashtra, India. The project has been jointly implemented by the Government of India through the National Informatics Centre, the Government of Maharashtra and the Warna Cooperative Society. This project was initiated to serve the information needs of the farmers for different crop cultivation practices of major crops, sugarcane cultivation practices, pest and disease control, marketing information, dairy and sugarcane processing information, and other agriculture-related services. Apart from information retrieval, there are two client based applications to serve the farmers' needs through the computer booths installed in each village:

- The Dairy Information Centre; and
- The Sugarcane Information System.

In the Dairy Information System, information on all farmers who are part of the dairy system is maintained. Other details available to members of the dairy co-operatives include the quantity of milk supplied by each farmer, fat content, billing information and credit details. This information is maintained and updated at the central database on a daily basis. In the Sugarcane Information System, information on shareholders is maintained. There are about 200-350 shareholders in each village for the sugarcane crop. This system maintains details of the cultivation schedule, the quantity harvested and supplied to the society, deductions effected by the society towards, credit, and the net income due to the farmers. This data is available with respect to each shareholder. Booth operators of Paragoam, Bhairwadi, Kuralap and Panhala report that an average of 20-25 farmers visit the computer booths every day for information on crop cultivation practices and disease control, marketing, dairy and sugarcane billing details, etc.

Creating Rural Knowledge Repositories

Tele-centers in Kannivadi and Samiarpatty developed a database on indigenous knowledge on issues such as livestock management, integrated pest management, the practices of the farmers in cultivating 42 crops focusing on pest and disease management. A database on the local expertise has been developed in the form of a rural yellow page. The information consists of consisting of names, addresses and information of various village professions such as blacksmiths, carpenters, plumbers, masons, nurses, traditional healers, etc. Similarly, a local consultant has been employed to gather information about all the development programmes in the region.

This database would provide the information regarding the objectives of the programmes, eligibility for participation, etc. Details of experts in agriculture and health are also kept in the tele-centers. Camps are organised where experts and villagers meet and discuss various issues in specific subjects. These discussions are captured in audiocassettes and video photography. In a form of question-answer, the discussions are kept in a database.

Camps such as livestock management, credit management, and women's health are being organised. through local area network. Moreover prints-out of some of the location-specific and very vital information are being pasted at the public places every day. Thus, Tagaval Thinnai is available both in 'online' form as well as in print form. The animators collect the information through formal channels such as web sites and informal channels such as contacting the traders. Some of the main sources of the information are agricultural extension agencies, the block development office, commission agents of the flower market at Nilakotai (a market town), Gandhigram, a deemed university etc. The information is collected and provided on a daily basis.

Local Web Sites

A local web site with the help of users of adult education centre can guide to relevant information. The web site can, on the one hand, be a medium for introducing information on the community with information provided by the community. On the other hand, the web site will provide links to useful information sources and present information that has been interpreted into the local languages. The web site can further link to online distance learning material and/or local databases.

Databases

The tele-center manager in collaboration with project volunteers can build their own databases. These shall be locally generated and, hence, locally and personally relevant information sources that can include details of government programmes for low-income rural families (dependent on the context of the particular community); local market prices for grain; local farming families; a directory of insurance plans for both crops and input prices; pest management plans for local products; a directory of local hospitals, medical practitioners and their specialities; a regional timetable for buses and trains; and a directory of local veterinarians, cattle, and animal husbandry programmes, etc. Databases could further include a collection of application software and reference material, such as CD ROMs relevant for responding to local needs. Most software producers donate license for their software to NGOs or community groups upon request, so if a NGO is in need of software, it can contact the producer.

Bulletin Boards

Bulletin boards present an easy-to-realise method of

presenting gathered information to a wide number of community members. Bulleting boards could be placed outside the adult education centre building and/or different focal points within the community and be updated regularly.

E-mail Lists

E-mail lists allow the posting of questions, receiving of news updates, and sharing of experiences via e-mail within a group that you define. An e-mail list is identified by a single name. A message is sent to the mailing list name and it is automatically forwarded or broadcast to all the addresses in the list. These mailing lists can be extremely helpful in connecting users of adult literacy programmes to share experiences. For example, Chasquinet, an Ecuador-based NGO, hosts a telecenter in Latin America and the Caribbean.

PARTICIPATION IN APPLICATION NETWORK

The participation in collaborative networks enables information to flow from and to rural communities, facilitates dialogue between communities, intermediaries and development organisations, fosters coordination of national and local development efforts and overcomes physical barriers to knowledge and information sharing. Networks provide information and help regarding particular topics, as well as access to the Internet, mail connections, radio connections, and e-mail. Generally, these applications use inexpensive storeand-forward systems to provide information on agriculture, public health, medicine, and the environment.

Example for an Application Network: FarmNet

Farmer Information Network (FarmNet) is a network of rural people and supporting intermediary organisations, such as extension services, using ICTs and conventional communication media to facilitate the generation, gathering and exchange of knowledge and information. Operated by farmers and their organisations, FarmNet links farmers to each other and to the resources and services, they need to improve their livelihoods. Design of a FarmNet with the Uganda

National Farmers' Association found that the best approach was to enhance existing communication efforts (face-to-face, local radio, publications) with the use of simple e-mail based communication system for information on markets, improved agricultural technologies and weather conditions.

5

Information Dissemination Services

INTRODUCTION

This chapter introduces the practical aspects of information dissemination. It will familiarize you with the techniques for finding out databases and thereby effectively retrieving the desired material. Further, it will describe the services you can use for information dissemination to adult community and discuss some of the document delivery services you can find in India and abroad. Our effort is to motivate you to use these services for obtaining documents not available at your adult learning setup. Small libraries in adult education and learning can utilize such services for acquiring documents not held in their own small collections.

THE COST OF ACCESS TO RESEARCH INFORMATION

Libraries are expensive and research libraries are particularly expensive. Even in the United States, few people can afford good access to primary scientific, medical, legal and scholarly information. Members of major universities have excellent library services. So do people who work in teaching hospitals, or for drug companies or rich law firms. Others have access to information only through the tedious, inefficient system of interlibrary lending. In less affluent countries the situation is worse; even the best universities cannot afford good libraries. Must access to scientific and professional information always be expensive, or is it possible that digital libraries might change this sad situation?

The costs of a conventional research library fall into three main categories: facilities (which include buildings), library materials and staff. In digital libraries, the facilities costs are small, since digital libraries avoid the need for expensive buildings. Digital libraries require computers and networks, but these are relatively inexpensive, and the costs to users are shared with other services, such as electronic mail and word processing.

To build digital libraries that are inexpensive for users requires dramatic reductions in the costs of materials and of staff. Progress is being made in reducing material costs. Open access materials on the Internet are making many primary materials available at no cost. Some open access materials are identical to those that are available commercially. Others provide an acceptable substitute, such as Amazon.com as an alternative to *Books in Print*. For several disciplines, the open access materials are already good enough to support research. In an earlier paper, I discussed the economic forms that are supporting these open access publications and the strong economic reasons to believe that the volume of open access materials will increase.

Hence, the key to inexpensive access to information lies in lower staff costs, which is the subject of this article. Big libraries are labor-intensive. Although salaries are low, staff costs are the largest item in most budgets, typically about half. The libraries at Harvard employ a thousand people and the Library of Congress more than four thousand. If professional and research information is to be available more widely, either users must bypass libraries, or libraries will have to employ fewer people. Over the past thirty-five years, libraries have automated routine clerical tasks, such as circulation or filing catalog cards. Is it possible that, at some future date, computers might assume the skilled tasks that now require professional librarians?

The term "automated digital library" can be used to describe a digital library where all tasks are carried out automatically. Computer programs substitute for the intellectually demanding tasks that are traditionally carried out by skilled professionals. These tasks include selection, cataloguing and indexing, seeking for information, reference services, and so on. The common theme is that these activities require considerable mental activity, the type of activity that people are skilled at and computers find difficult. Automated digital libraries should not be confused with library automation, which uses computing to reduce routine tasks in conventional libraries.

EQUIVALENT LIBRARY SERVICES

The remainder of this chapter discusses the question of whether automated digital libraries can give good service to users. The short answer is that many aspects of automated libraries are a mirage — always just over the horizon — but some are surprisingly close or actually with us today. The underlying question is not whether automated digital libraries can rival conventional digital libraries today. They clearly cannot. The question is whether we can conceive of a time (perhaps twenty years from now) when they will provide an acceptable substitute.

Quality of service in automated digital libraries will not come from replicating the procedures of classical librarianship. More likely, automated libraries will provide users with equivalent services that are fundamentally different in the way that they are delivered. For example, within the foreseeable future, computer programs are unlikely to be much good at applying the Anglo American Cataloguing Rules to monographs. But cataloguing rules are a means to an end, not the end itself. They exist to provide services to users, notably information discovery. Automatic methods for information discovery may not need traditional cataloguing rules. The criterion for evaluating the new methods is whether the users find what the information that they require.

Consider the contrast between web search engines and conventional abstracting and indexing services or library catalogs. Almost everything that is best about a library catalog is done badly by a web search service. The selection of which materials to index by a web search engine relies on arbitrary considerations, the indexing records are crude at best, authority control is non-existent, and the elimination of duplicates leaves much to be desired. On the other hand, web search services are strong in ways that catalogs are weak. While cataloguing is expensive, indexing the web is cheap. The leading web search engines index several hundred million web pages every month, more than the total number of MARC records that have ever been created. It is wrong to claim that conventional catalogs or indexes are superior because of their quality control, and it is equally wrong to claim that the web search services are superior because of their coverage and currency. The value to users depends on what the user wants to achieve.

For medical research, no web search engine can approach the National Library of Medicine's Medline service. Medline has over 11 million references and abstracts. It is built by a team of indexers who have knowledge of bio-medical research, using indexing rules and MeSH subject headings that have been developed laboriously over decades. In contrast, web search services such as Google^{SM} are entirely automated. The indexes are built by a team of computers with no knowledge of what they are indexing. Google has the advantage over Medline of indexing hundreds of millions of web pages, and doing so repeatedly every month. It is quite useful for finding general information on medical topics, but it does not index the major scientific journals, its indexing records are crude, it has no understanding of medical terminology, and makes no attempt to separate sound medicine from quackery. It is a long way from being a substitute for Medline.

On the other hand, consider the trade-off between Google and Inspec, which is the leading abstracting and indexing service for computing. I used to be a regular user of Inspec, but have largely abandoned it in favor of Google. In many areas of computing, Google's restriction to open access web materials is relatively unimportant, since almost every significant result first appears on a web site and only later reaches the printed journals, if ever. Google is more up to date than Inspec, its coverage is broader and its indexing records are good enough for me to find what I am looking for. But its greatest strength is that everything in its indexes is available online with open access. In computing, substantially the same information is often available from several sources. Google provides a direct link to an open access version. Inspec references a formally published version, which is usually printed or online with restricted access. For my purposes, Google's broad coverage and convenient links more than compensate for its weaknesses.

This discussion highlights important differences between disciplines. For example, a scientist judges a library catalog simply as a tool for information discovery, while, for a humanist, the catalog may be a bibliographic source in its own right. Any predictions of the future value of web search engines compared with conventional abstracting and indexing services depend heavily on the publication and reading habits of people in different disciplines. However, as we look ahead twenty years, the most difficult part of the comparison is to guess how the automated tools will develop. We know that they will improve dramatically and we can anticipate that research habits will accommodate themselves to the new tools, but only a fool would attempt to forecast the precise changes that will occur.

BRUTE FORCE COMPUTING

The first serious study of what is here called automated digital libraries was at MIT in the 1960s, under the leadership of J. C. R. Licklider, and discussed in his 1965 book "Libraries of the Future" . This remarkable book described the design of what he called "procognitive systems" for the year 2000. It envisaged digital libraries based around "information-processing schemata" that would be free from the physical constraints of books and library shelves. He listed twenty-five desiderata listed for procognitive systems. Many of these are definitely in the realm of artificial intelligence. For example, one of his desiderata was, "Converse or negotiate with the user while he formulates his requests and while responding to them."

At the time that Licklider was writing, early experiments in artificial intelligence showed great promise in imitating human processes with simple algorithms. (For a contemporary view of this work, see Feigenbaum and Feldman, "Computers and Thought".) Therefore, Licklider was optimistic that, within thirty years, advanced algorithms in fields such as natural language understanding would enable intellectual processes to be carried out automatically.

Thirty-five years later, we can see that many of the results that he predicted have come to fruition, but not all and not in the manner that he expected. The development of sophisticated natural language processing has been slower than hoped, with general-purpose software still on the distant horizon. However, while Licklider and his contemporaries were over-optimistic about the development of sophisticated methods of artificial intelligence, they underestimated how much could be achieved by brute force computing, in which vast amounts of computer power are used with simple algorithms.

The rate of progress in computing power is described by Moore's Law, that the number of transistors on a semiconductor doubles every eighteen months. This is roughly equivalent to saying that computing power increases 100-fold in 10 years or 10,000-fold in 20 years. Few people can appreciate the implications of such dramatic change, but the future of automated digital libraries is likely to depend more on brute force computing than on sophisticated algorithms.

Many of the most successful methods of artificial intelligence apply simple methods to huge volumes of data. An interesting example comes from the computer programs that play chess. The IBM system that is now equal to the world's greatest grandmasters is descended from Deep Thought, a student project at Carnegie Mellon University. The members of the Deep Thought team were not chess experts. Their breakthrough came from expertise in developing exceptionally fast hardware, which could analyze immense numbers of chess variations.

The potential for automated digital libraries lies in the simple observation that:

> *Simple algorithms plus immense computing power often outperform human intelligence.*

Moore's Law tells us that the computing power will be available.

The State-of-the-Art in Automated Digital Libraries

The introduction of automated digital libraries is a continual process, much of it happening outside conventional libraries. Here are some current examples.

Information Discovery

Information discovery illustrates the complementary skills of computers and people. Humans are skilled at reading a few thousand words and extracting complex concepts. Faced with a billion pages (roughly the size of the web), they are helpless. Computers can index every word in a billion pages and search the indexes for simple patterns almost instantaneously.

The web search services represent the state-of-the-art in automated information discovery. Within each service lie a number of separate processes, each of which is carried out automatically, and each of which is constrained by the current state of computing. To build the indexes, a web crawler must decide which pages to index, eliminate duplicates, create a short index record for each page and add the terms found on the page to its inverted files. To search the index, the search engine must convert the user's query to a search command, match it against the inverted files, rank the results and return them to the user.

To anticipate the potential of automatic systems to rival the functionality of Medline in all disciplines, we need to examine the components of a system like Google and see how they could be improved. Moore's law predicts that computers will be 10,000 times more powerful in twenty years. With such computer power available, we know that the automatic search systems will be extremely good, even if no new algorithms are invented.

For example, to decide how closely a document matches a query would seem to require human judgment, yet standard methods of information retrieval do remarkably well. They use the power of computers to match simple patterns as a surrogate for the human ability to relate concepts. As humans, we use our understanding of language to observe that two texts are on similar topics, or to rank how closely documents match a query. Computers can estimate closeness of match by comparing word frequencies. One basic concept, developed by Gerald Salton at Cornell University about 1970, represents each document as a multi-dimensional vector and uses the angle between their vectors as a measure of the similarity of two documents.

Evaluating the importance of documents would appear to be another task that requires human understanding, but Google's ranking algorithm does remarkably well entirely automatically. The idea behind this algorithm is simple. Google ranks web pages by how many other pages link to them. It gives greater weight to links from higher-ranking pages. Calculating the ranks requires the algorithm to iterate through a matrix that has as many rows and columns as there are pages on the web, yet with modern computing and considerable ingenuity, Google performs this calculation routinely. As a result, Google is remarkably successful in presenting a user with the most important page on a topic or a well-respected overview. This algorithm was developed as part of the NSF-funded Digital Library Initiative.

Archiving and Preservation

The Internet Archive, directed by Brewster Kahle, provides a topical example of the economic advantages of automated digital libraries. The Internet is an extremely important part of modern culture and contains many materials that should be preserved for future generations. Each month, a web crawler gathers every open access web page with associated images. The Internet Archive preserves these files for the future and mounts them on computers available for scholarly research today.

The Internet Archive is not perfect. Only HTML pages and images are collected, no Java applets or style sheets; the materials are dumped into a computer system with no organization or indexing; broken links are left broken; and access for scholars is rudimentary. Yet the simple fact is that without the automated approach of the Internet Archive, these materials would already have been lost. Attempts to catalog and collect web materials using skilled librarians and archivists have floundered on the scale of effort needed to do even a rudimentary job.

Citations, Hyperlinks and Reference Linking

Citation analysis is a long-standing success story of applying computers to library information. Inspired by the efforts of Eugene Garfield, the founder of Science Citation Index, there is a long tradition of using citations as bibliographic measures. Hyperlinks are the web's equivalent to citations. Since they are already in machine-readable form, they are amenable to algorithmic analysis. Google's ranking algorithm can be seen as applying the concepts of citation analysis to the web.

Hyperlinks refer to items or copies of a work, but citations normally refer to the work itself or a specific manifestation. Automatic systems are becoming capable of extracting a reference from a document and linking it to the digital object that it references.

Reference linking is one of the building blocks that are being used to build large-scale automated digital libraries. ResearchIndex is a digital library of computer science materials, created entirely automatically by Steve Lawrence and colleagues at NEC. It makes extensive use of citation analysis and reference linking. It downloads papers from the web. If they are in PostScript or PDF, it converts them to text. It parses the papers to extract citations and the context for the citation. It provides users with services such as searching the entire text or the citations, listing the references within a paper, following the citation links, or displaying the context in which references appear. An interesting aspect of ResearchIndex is that it provides a way for users to submit corrections, automatically of course.

Beyond Text

Metadata is one of the foundations of librarianship. There are a number of projects that extract metadata from digital objects automatically. Perhaps the most remarkable is the Informedia project, led by Howard Wactlar at Carnegie Mellon University. Informedia has the extremely ambitious goal of providing access to segments of video, such as television news, entirely automatically. Thus it includes algorithms for dividing raw video into discrete items, for generating short summaries (called "skims"), for indexing the sound track using speech recognition, for recognizing faces and for searching using methods of natural language processing. Each of these methods is a tough research topic and, not surprisingly, Informedia provides only a rough-and-ready service, but overall it is surprisingly effective. Moreover, many of the weaknesses of Informedia could be overcome by applying huge amounts of computing power. Informedia was another project of the Digital Library Initiative.

SEARCH STRATEGY

Search strategy is about formulating search statement for an effective retrieval and about deciding the databases as such suitable for searching and retrieval. It is all about series of operations and decisions starting from developing an understanding of user's needs to selecting appropriate databases for retrieval, formulating search statement by using suitable keywords, descriptors and phrases (reflecting user's requirements) coupled with or without Boolean operators, and the data fields on which to carryout the search. The role of the library is to mediate between the user and the information resources, working out a plan of action from amongst the various available options for database searching. Retrieval performance is all about postsearch operations involving evaluation of the search output for its relevance to the user's needs and revising search strategy in the light of the user's feedback.

USER'S REQUIREMENTS

In mediated searching, understanding user's requirements is about bridging the gap between the 'expressed needs' and 'actual need'. The gap sometimes stems from the lack of understanding of the part of the user about terms and keywords used in the database to express a key concept under retrieval. The best approach to reduce this gap is to ask the user to provide a few references of documents that seem to meet his expressed requirements. You could use the keywords used to index such documents in the database to understand his 'actual requirements'. The second approach to reducing the gap is to expose the user to descriptors in the thesaurus and to let him express his requirements using descriptors relevant to his topic.

SELECTING DATABASE

Selection of a database for retrieval depends upon the subject of the query and specialty of the database. It also depends upon depth and breadth of coverage of indexed resources in the database, coverage of indexed resources by regions and countries, and accessibility to database archive for retrospective searching and full-text searching.

QUERY FORMULATION OPTIONS

A search query can be simple or compound. In addition, you can advance a search by using Boolean, limiting, string, proximity and truncation operators and sets. As suggested, now discuss each type of query formulation options.

Simple Query

In simple query, you use only keywords (or descriptors taken from the controlled vocabulary). Sometimes, you may use a phrase in place of keywords in the simple query. In such a case, you will retrieve only records matching the phrase. However, you reduce the chances of finding records matching the query if phrase is quite long. In case, you use only keywords for expressing the query (i.e. without using any operator); the search output would comprise records containing one or more keywords matching the query.

Thus, the greater the number of keywords in the query the larger would be size of the search output. There is no single formula for keeping the output small when there are too many keywords in query. Thus the tip to searching nearly exact match is to keep the query as simple as possible but without losing specificity in expressing the query.

Compound Query

One of the strategies to keep the acφ search output (matching the query) small is to construct a compound query using Boolean operators. OR, AND, NOT. You can use them to group search terms to broaden or narrow the results of a search.

Boolean searching is a method of combining search terms either to retrieve more documents (use OR as the Boolean operator) or a smaller and more precise set of documents (use AND or NOT as the Boolean operator). Most databases and search engines allow Boolean searching, but may also use special characters or commands. AND retrieves items in which both terms are found, *e.g.*, adult AND community. OR retrieves items in which either term is found, *e.g.*, adult OR community. NOT retrieves items in which the first term is present but the second term is not *e.g.* information NOTt knowledge. In other words AND narrows a search, OR expands a search, and NOT excludes terms from the search.

Advanced Search

Simple or compound search can be further refined by combining advanced search capabilities of the search engine such as limiting the search to specific fields in the record, grouping keywords in the query statement, using proximity operators, truncation features etc,

Limiting Search

Many search engines provide the facility to limit the search to any one or more fields, say, title, author, descriptors, language, publication year, and country of publication.

String Search

Many search engines allow searching data fields for

character strings that are not in the index. For example, character string 'adult education and learning' can be searched by employing string search technique. This facility is particularly useful in searching for specific characters.

Proximity Search

Proximity operator between two terms is used to find records that contain both terms in the same field. For example, when searching for 'adult WITH literacy', the word and word literacy would both appear in the same search field. This operator can thus be used to make a search more precise than using the AND operator. Some search engines use the term 'SAME' in place of 'WITH' to represent proximity operator.

Order of Precedence when Using Multiple Operators

Parentheses override the order of precedence when using multiple Boolean and/ or Proximity operators. The search statement "house* and (finance$ or loan$)" retrieves documents that contain some variant of the word house and either one (or both) of the terms in the parenthesis. You can use up to fifty search operators in a single search statement. The order of precedence for multiple operators would be as follows:

- ( )
- Same/ With
- NOT
- AND
- OR

Truncation

Truncation can be used in a number of different ways:

- At the end of the word to retrieve all mentions of the word (singular and plural), all forms of a root in cases of irregular plurals, and to retrieve more than one character, and
- Internal truncation or wildcard characters to retrieve alternate spellings of words.

You may apply truncation at least after three characters. The truncation symbol * serves as a substitute for any string of zero or more characters. The wildcard symbol '?' serves as a substitute for any one character exactly. For example, the search for wom?n retrieves woman or women. One can use truncation or wildcards anywhere in the search term except as the first character. The wildcard symbol $ serves as a substitute for zero or one character.

- $ = zero or one character
- * = Zero or more characters
- ? = one character only

PRECISION

It is a ratio of relevant records retrieved (relevant hits = total records retrieved –noise) to total records retrieved (hits + noise). It is computed as (A/G). It measures the ability of the system to suppress noise in the search output.

	Retrived	Not Retrieved	Total
Relevant	A (HITS)	B (Missed)	C
Non-Relevant	D (Noised)	X	
Total	G	H	

Precision

You can obtain user feedback in terms of recall and precision taken as the basis for improving retrieval performance by suitably amending search statement in the query.

INFORMATION SERVICES

The libraries could use in-house databases as well as external bibliographic and full-text databases for organising information dissemination services. In adult education and learning sector the constituencies that need library support and services are two:

1. Adult community and
2. Academic and research teams planning and organising adult education programmes.

The most common service that libraries have been offering over the years is the access to document collections. However, the expectations of both the constituencies from the libraries go far beyond the accessibility to internal collections. The adult community is more interested in getting useful information than just the documents. Given their low socioeconomic status and their low literacy level, they need practical and processed information useful in making informed choices or taking decisions on matters relating to their livelihood and living standard, and guarding themselves against exploitation and deprivation, etc.

The other constituency in the adult education and learning sector, which comprises academic and research teams, needs services far beyond the accessibility to document collections. They need bibliographic information, condensed information, analytical information, repackaged information, and consolidated information and such other content-oriented information for understanding latest developments in the field, state-of-the-art in the subject, and complete overview of the topic.

TYPES OF LIBRARY AND INFORMATION SERVICE

Broadly, libraries offer different types of library and information services that should be of relevance to both the user constituencies in the adult education sector. These services include:

- Current Information,
- Everyday Use Information,
- Catching up information services, and
- Exhaustive Information.

CURRENT INFORMATION SERVICES

Such services usually refer to keeping up to date with the latest literature published/ information in a subject area for the adult community in rural areas 'mandi' (wholesale market) rates for farm produce, revision in loan rates from the banks, latest health and family planning programmes, agricultural melas (fairs), etc constitute current information as it is crucliterature, store it first in the database, before disseminating it to the adult community. However, for the academic and research teams engaged in adult education and learning programmes, the connotation of current information is different.

To them it implies latest research papers and publications in journals, latest books and monographs in the field, pre-prints, etc. The purpose of such a service is to understand current research trends in the field and to gain knowledge about the highest level of achievements in the field. For planning and organising current information services, the libraries need to browse published and grey literature in adult education and learning, and compile the relevant data in the database for producing such services as Current Titles service (classified by subject) and Table of Contents service (organised by journal titles). In addition, there are also:

- Selective Dissemination of Information (customised to individual's needs) and
- Electronic Clipping Service. About the latter two services, as suggested, discuss a little more.

Selective Dissemination of Information (Customised to Individual's Needs)

In addition, the library can organise selective dissemination of information (SDI) wherein the current information is provided to the users on the select topics of interests to the users, and from select sources of information. The user feedback is an important pre-requisite in the SDI service as it helps in performance evaluation of the SDI service and introducing midcourse changes, if so required, in the user profile or the search query for improved performance.

Electronic Clipping Service

Electronic publishers provide electronic clipping service to individual users on select topics of their interest. Individuals need to register with the publishers for the service. They get in their mail box listings of research papers from current issues of journals and on the subject of their interest. This service is now a substitute for the traditional current awareness services as well as SDI service.

EVERYDAY INFORMATION SERVICE

It is about information needed for performing day-to-day activities such as conducting experiments, engineering operations in a factory, fabricating products, etc. Usually reference sources such as directories, handbooks, and encyclopaedias are of used in giving such type of information services. The need for such type of information services for adult community is usually not very strong.

CATCHING UP INFORMATION SERVICE

In this service, complete picture on a particular topic in given in simple and short form to enable an individual to catch up and comprehend the developments in the subject since the time he lost touch in it.

Such a service includes:

- Popular write-ups on a subject/ topic on demand,
- Contents that empower adult learners and enable them to understand the importance of information/ knowledge, and
- Knowledge and information useful for economic activity.

EXHAUSTIVE INFORMATION SERVICE

Exhaustive information services are important for assessing and understanding overall developments in the subject. These services include literature search, bibliography compilations, and state of the art reports, critical reviews, etc. You can customise such services to individual's needs and give them on demand. Coverage of information in such a service is exhaustive. Usually such services are of importance and relevance in knowledge creation and utilisation and as such useful and relevant to adult education teams.

DOCUMENT DELIVERY SYSTEMS AND SERVICES

Libraries supporting adult education and learning programmes are required to provide documents on demand or in support of pro-active services that they organise. Given the fact that the collections size of NGO libraries is usually not large, they may not be able to provide access to all documents on demand from their in-house collections. They will have to depend upon external document delivery systems for the purpose. Initially, before the advent of photocopying machine, libraries used to exchange documents in their holdings on demand on inter-library loan. However, with the advent of photocopying machines, photocopies have replaced the practice of lending original documents.

The end users or user libraries get photocopies of documents for permanent retention. Subsequently, with the emergence of electronic publishing era and advent of ICT, Internet era, the libraries started sharing their resources by transmitting digital images of the print documents or sending electronic files of digital documents over the Internet.

In the literature, the terms 'inter-library loan' and 'document delivery' are used interchangeably. However, the two terminologies have specific and different connotations though they serve to meet the same end purpose. In inter-library loan, you can borrow only holdings of the library such as books, journals, reports, standards, etc., from one library to another but for a limited period only. You need to return such documents to the lending library after the expiry of loan period. In inter-library loan, you never get documents for permanent retention. On the other hand, in document delivery, the end-user gets copies of the documents such as photocopies/ electronic images/ fax images/ electronic files for permanent retention.

MODES OF DOCUMENT DELIVERY SERVICE

Document delivery means supplying documents on demand in either original or as copies of the original (copies in print or digital format) and delivered through mail/ courier or over communication networks. Document delivery to end users implies three types of operations:

1. Document identification,
2. Document location, and
3. Document procurement.

Document identification requires verifying the bibliographical elements of the documents to ensure that details such as author, article title, source title, volume, and pages as given in the user request are correct. You can verify such details by searching the Web or the relevant databases. Document location implies identifying the library holdings the documents under reference. You may do this by searching union catalogues available from library networks. Document procurement implies writing to the relevant libraries/ service providers for delivery documents. There are several modes of document procurement.

- Requesting documents from the holdings library/ library networks
- Requesting documents from document delivery service providers
- Searching the Web for digital copies of the documents for free access

DOCUMENT DELIVERY SERVICE PROVIDERS

There are several document service providers in India and abroad. Their role is to provide copies of documents on demand. The mode of copying may be photocopy, fax image, digital image, or duplicate electronic file. The delivery options are post-mail, courier, fax, or over the network. Unlike traditional libraries which give documents without charging any money, these delivery systems are commercial in approach and charge for providing document delivery service. These systems compete with each other in terms of speed of service, being exhaustive in terms of depth and breadth of information sources, and in terms of service costs.

6

Databases

DESIGN AND DEVELOPMENT OF WEB-ENABLED DATABASES

Application of computers certainly has improved the ways in which we acquire, process, store and disseminate information in libraries. As a result, we have automated house-keeping operations, catalogue and, user services in libraries. Moreover, with the advancement in the network technology during last decade, we have started providing user services through various online modes, *viz.*, e-mail, FTP, Telnet, etc. These static/ interactive modes of data/information sharing over network have improved the library services and, their popularity among the users. During 1994, libraries began to show their presence on the internet by setting up their web sites.

In the beginning, libraries built their web pages by providing mainly static information. However, in the late 1997, libraries began re-engineering their web pages with the intention of providing information from databases in a dynamic manner. Today the advancements in web and database technology have enabled the libraries to share/ publish the data/information directly from the databases over the internet.

Now web has become a dynamic platform for information delivery over the internet and very useful for libraries to provide various user services. This chapter intends to provide an overview of the database tools available for designing in-house databases in the libraries as well as the web technology for publishing such databases over the web. Besides, the paper discusses the need of developing in-house databases in libraries, advantages of web-enabled databases, and selection of database tools from RDBMS commonly available.

IN-HOUSE DATABASES IN LIBRARIES

There are a number of ready-made library automation software packages in the market which can be used to automate the library functions and user services. However, many of these packages lack web interface and, thus, do not provide library database access (OPAC, etc.) through web. Moreover, these commercial packages provide less flexibility to librarians for making desired changes to the existing databases and to publish the same on the web. An in-house designed database system provides full flexibility to the developer/administrator/librarian and is simpler to install, maintain and, use without having to rely on external support, and also is highly customisable and can be designed to meet local needs.

Librarians can also participate in design/development process as now a days easy and user-friendly database tools are available with in-built web interface. As per the survey conducted in order to get a clear understanding of the current role of library web master, 100 percent of the respondents felt that librarians should have some role in web site design and maintenance.

BENEFITS OF WEB-ENABLED DATABASES

Web-enabled databases have certain advantages over other means of sharing/publishing information over internet. These advantages are common to bibliographic databases also where libraries can put their OPACs and other databases on web.

The benefits of web-enabled databases are as follows:

- Global/wide ac cess to data with a sin gle user in ter face
- Format in dependent ac cess of data (text, graph ics, au dio, video, etc.)
- Up-to-minute up dated ac cess of data in real time
- Dynamic updation of data from many locations

- Cost-effective way of data sharing
- Instant feedback from users
- Seamless links from resource to resource
- Unlimited download/printing
- Environmental friendly.

Besides, Ortiz-Repiso and Norm Medeiros have written excellent papers on differences between traditional v/s innovative means (web OPACs) of library catalogs, while B. Ramesh Babu, *et al* have presented an overview of web OPACS with their advantages in libraries.

DATABASE TOOLS

In the early days of database development, it was the flat-file system to store data in a single file by using field separators and record separators. Later, such flat-file systems were facilitated by an index in which a single index file stored keywords and pointers to the records that were stored in main file.

This made retrieval more efficient, still flat-file systems were seriously inefficient. It showed data-redundancy, poor data control, and did not supported complex data types (audio, video, graphics, etc.). After 1960s, two database models were developed in quick succession to solve the limitations of flat-file systems.

These database models were Hierarchical Database Model and Network Database Model. The Hierarchical Database composes of a root segment, parent segments and child segments.

This model depicts a set of one-to-many relationships between a parent and its children. However, this model has number of limitations. It does not include *ad hoc* querying capability and, a multi-parent relationship is difficult to implement, as in a many-to-many relationship. The Network Database Model attempted to deal with many of the hierarchical model's limitations. The network database structure easily accommodates the multiple child, although, its structural complexities often limit its effectiveness and efficiency. Both of these database models are obsolete now mainly because of their incompatibility with web environment and have been replaced by RDBMS.

RDBMS is the current database implementation standard being used for publishing information on the web. It includes the following features which make it suitable for web environment:

- Provide extremely useful tools for databaseadministration;
- Adhere to powerful query language SQL (structured query language) developed by Microsoft Corporation;
- Compliant with ODBC/JDBC and other database interface tools;
- Work in client/server mode;
- Offer distributed database and distributed processing options; and
- Have referential integrity controls to ensure data consistency and, thus, suitable for web environment.

It is easier to design applications in RDBMS due to the following features:

- Requires less programming skill
- Availability of third party tools, and
- Inbuilt web interface.

These all features of RDBMS have made them ideal for library applications to setup bibliographic database solutions and publishing them over the web. In the early days of library systems development, vendors have designed library applications software by using pre-relational database technology.

Still some library systems suppliers are continuing to maintain and develop such products. These proprietary library applications software have their own advantages and disadvantages. However, in the library management systems marketplace, there is a growing trend towards the use of RDBMS as shown in Fig. 6.1 and Fig. 6.2.

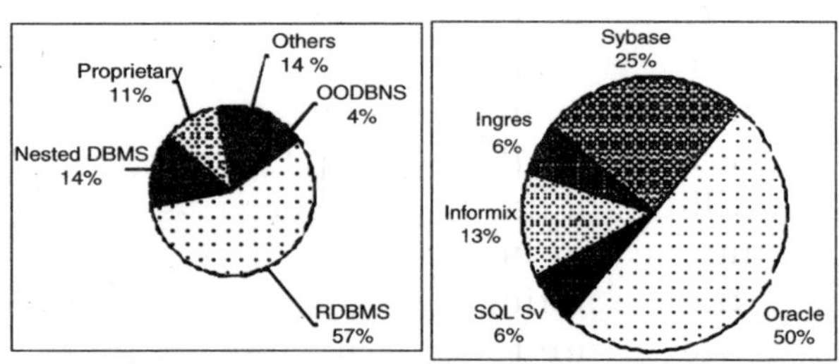

Fig 6.1 Type of Databases **Fig 6.2 Use of Various RDBMS in Library Used in Library Systems**

As per the Gartner list of database management systems, there are 140 products from 67 vendors ranging from pre-relational, relational and, object-oriented databases (OODBMS). The RDBMS accounted three-quarters of the total database market.

Table 6.1 Market Percentage of Vendors in DBMS Sector

Company	2000 Market (%)	1999 Market (%)
Oracle	33.8	31.4
IBM	30.1	29.9
Microsoft	14.9	13.1
Sybase	3.2	3.3
Informix	3.0	5.0
Others	15.0	17.3

Table shows that in the relational segment, there are 'Big Five' DBMS vendors which include Oracle, IBM, Microsoft, Informix, and Sybase

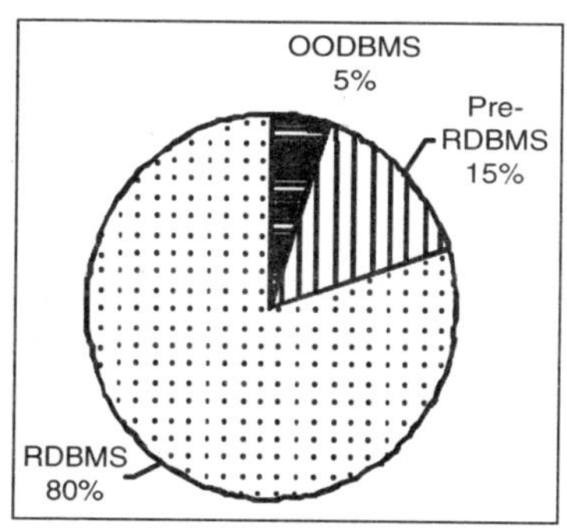

Fig 6.3 Worldwide DBMS New Licence Revenue

Some of the common RDBMS which can be used to design in-house databases in libraries are *MS Access, SQL Server, Oracle, Informix, Sybase, File Maker Pro, SAS,* etc. However, the selection of suitable RDBMS for library applications depends on the particular library requirements, kind of applications (bibliographic/full-text/numeric), the application level (database level/data warehouse level), magnitude of data (number of records/length of fields), nature of data analysis (basic statistics, *i.e.*, sum, average, mean/advance statistics) and, comprehensiveness and inter-operability.

Other points to be considered while selecting database tools for library applications are easiness, user-friendliness, flexibility and low cost. In most of the cases in libraries where bibliographic databases are dealt with, commonly available consumer database products such as *MS Access*, and *File Maker Pro* are sufficient. These products can support up to 1GB of data and provide cheaper solutions. However, these database tools are suitable for small databases and not useful for large databases, hence provide limitations in web environment. There are specific database solutions for large databases available from *MS SQL Server, DB2, Oracle, Informix, Sybase,* etc.

These database tools support up to several terra byte of data; permit thousands of simultaneous users; work in client/server mode; show natural affinity towards web environment and, thus, suitable for large bibliographic, web-enabled databases in libraries. However, to design full-text databases in libraries where large files are to be stored and retrieved, these tools do not offer good solutions as most of these tools support 200-255-400 characters field length. Although, many of these tools allow unlimited entries in memo field, the data inside a memo field are not searchable and thus, offer limited utility. In this respect, *MS SQL Server* has extended the searchable field length up to 8063 characters and thus, provide solutions for moderate full-text databases.

As a common trend, a number of libraries have been using open source software available either free or on nominal prices. These database management systems include the most common *mySQL, mSQL* and, recently updated *PostgreSQL.* These database tools are easy to work and run on various platforms such as UNIX, Lynux, NT, etc. Besides, there are some library specific text retrieval database tools for management of full-text large files, generally known as 'Free Form Databases', provide powerful search engine.

Although, in some ways they are at the opposite end of the RDBMS, little database structure imposed on the designer and, thus, provide an easy and readymade database structure. However, they provide some limitations in achieving integration in the modules other than searching such as cataloguing, classification, management module, etc. These software are *BRS/Search, Basis Plus, Status,* etc.

WEB TECHNOLOGY

World Wide Web or WWW or web, sometimes wrongly mentioned as synonymous to internet, is a sub-set of it and is a most promising mode of publishing/sharing of data/ information. Now, the web has emerged as the dominant protocol over internet due to its special features like easy interfacing of diverse platforms/technologies; provision to incorporate text, graphics, audio and video, etc.; permitting to access data/information in a non-linear way and; jumping from one document/resource to another through hyperlinks.

The superiority of www over other modes of online sharing, *viz.*, e-mail, FTP, Telnet, Gopher, etc., has been well explained by Paul Scully. In fact, web has provided a single user interface to facilitate the user interaction with the databases or systems resources. The web uses unique URL (universal resource locator) address which facilitates the access of information seamlessly across the diverse platforms in a client-server mode.

The actual data represented in a structured way reside in a powerful computers called server, while the latter is equipped with server tools/software to populate the information over web. The client/user equipped with web browser such as Microsoft Internet Explorer (MSIE) and Netscape Navigator, etc., which interact with the server through common communications protocol TCP/IP over high speed network/internet. In fact, the client/user sends its query to the server while the latter processes the request and gets the response/results from the database and sends it back to the client/user over the web.

COMPONENTS OF WEB-BASED SYSTEMS

Following components are required for web-based systems:

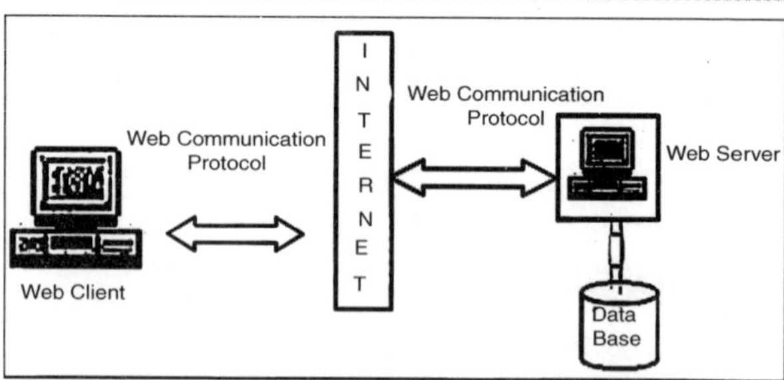

Fig 6.4 World Wide Web Architecture

Web Browser

It is a software that helps users to interact with the server for sending queries and getting results over the web. MSIE and Netscape are the most popular web browsers, both of these are available free.

Web Server

Web server is the software that helps in sharing the system resources/files over the internet through web browsers. The latter communicate with a web server via the standard Hyper-Text Transfer Protocol (HTTP). In fact, web servers receive queries from the client, process it, get data from databases and send it back to the client over web.

The popular web servers are Apache, Microsoft IIS, iPlanet from Sun-Netscape alliance, and newly developed *Zeus* from Zeus Technology Ltd. Although web servers are increasingly found as components within full-featured server operating systems, there are some basic selection points that should be highlighted.

These points are scalability and performance; high availability and reliability; interoperability and open standards; system administration and; security. In fact, there are not much choice in the web server segments as many of them come along with database tools, show natural affinity with the database tools from same vendor, and some other work better with certain platform/operating systems. The widely followed Netcraft web survey, approximately 60 percent of web servers run Apache, with Microsoft's IIS and the Netscape/iPlanet web server as its major competitors. However, Gartner studies have given Netscape/iPlanet a larger share of public web sites, followed by Apache and Microsoft/IIS.

Apache is being used for the public sites of companies such as Merck, American Express, Texaco, Chrysler, and others. However, it is easier to find both Microsoft/IIS and Netscape/iPlanet as the servers for large corporate public web sites when using the lookup facility offered by Netcraft. Also, for intranets, most counts credit Microsoft/IIS and Netscape/iPlanet as the leaders, followed by Apache, IBM's Lotus Domino Go server, and others. Among hot e-commerce sites, E*Trade runs the Netscape/iPlanet server, eBay runs Windows/IIS, and Amazon runs Apache (the Apache-based Stronghold Secure Server).

WEB AUTHORING TOOLS

Basic web server software does nothing except it sends HTML data in response to a browser request. However, certain other web-authoring and scripting tools are required to extend the functionality of web server to extract the data from databases. These web-authoring tools (*HTML* and its derivatives; and other Markup languages, etc.) and scripting tools (*Perl, C++, Java Script, JScript, VBScript,* etc.) are required to write web pages and scripts to interact with back-end databases.

In early days of web-based applications, *CGI* (common gateway interface) programmes were used extensively to extend the server functionality by allowing web users to interact with the web server to request specific data from the databases.

Although, writing *CGI* programme is difficult and requires programming skill, however, it works with high reliability. Now a days, a number visual editors are available to generate the web pages and write scripts automatically. The common editors are *Microsoft Front Page, Visual Interdev, Netscape Composer, Web Builder,* etc. Besides, other technologies have been introduced to communicate with the back-end databases.

These technologies are Microsoft *Active Server Pages (ASP)* and *Java Server Pages (JSP)* from Sun Micro Systems. Both the technologies have combined the HTML codes with the scripts in a single page and thus, making it easier to interact with back-end databases. During last few years, object-oriented and component based solutions were added to further make it easier to interact with the back-end databases. These solutions include:

- Microsoft COM/DCOM,
- ActiveX Data Objects (ADO);
- OMA and CORBA (Common Objects Request Broker Architecture) from Object Management Group;
- Sun's EJB (Enterprise Java Beans),
- Java Applets (for client) and
- Java Servlets (for server), etc.

Besides, some database connectivity tools such as ODBC and JDBC have also emerged as in-built features of operating systems, etc.

FREE WIZARDS AND THIRD PARTY TOOLS

Writing HTML codes and scripts for database interaction is the most difficult part, requires programming skill, systems logic and manipulation planning, especially for non-computer professionals. However, a number of free wizards and third party tools are available on internet which can generate hundred of lines of codes automatically with a single click, thus, making it easier for non-skilled users to set up web-enabled database solutions in libraries. Some of the free wizards are Rule Zero, Power ASP, Active Server Pages Tools and Components, etc. Besides, *Microsoft FrontPage* also provides database wizard to generate *ASP* pages/*VBScripts* automatically to interact with back-end databases, while *Visual InterDev* provides a visual interface to develop a web-enabled web site with minimum efforts.

DATABASE SEARCHING IN CENTRAL UNIVERSITY LIBRARIES IN INDIA

In consequence of the recommendation of the National

Knowledge Commission, each of the Indian states has at least one fully-funded central university. Now there are 39 central universities. Privately funded and owned statelegislated universities are also being established to cater to the increased demand for higher education. In between there are many universities that are not legislation-based but are authorised by the University Grant Commission to award degrees. Central universities are better-equipped in terms of financial resources, faculty, and infrastructure, and thus have an edge over the usually fund-starved state universities.

The libraries across the globe are challenged to integrate e-resources into their collection, services, and patrons' lives and academic libraries face obstacles when virtual learning environment (VLEs) become "the primary means of interaction between students and universities. Providing access to electronic journals and other e-resources is an important area of librarianship. The design of usable online interfaces is a crucial issue. Traditional library services and printed material are still more effective to researchers in Indian universities than web-based information and resources. Barriers to progress in this area in university libraries in India cannot be overlooked.

NETWORK INFRASTRUCTURE AND STRENGTH

Fast and effective information retrieval to support information sharing requires sound and wide network with adequate bandwidth. The UGC-sponsored Infonet is the mainstay of the academic info-network infrastructure. The UGC has constituted a national committee called the Central Monitoring Committee (CMC) for smooth implementation and execution of information infrastructure.

The CMC has chosen ERNET India (Education and Research Network) to establish information network in universities. The committee has recommended high bandwidth campus wide networks for Internet and external connectivity. So far 149 universities have been provided connectivity with raw bandwidth ranging from 512 KBPS to 20 MBPS. The Inflibnet is administering and funds its cost for all these universities.

ONLINE DATABASES

Out of the eight universities surveyed, seven are members of the UGC-Infonet consortia. The IGNOU, due to its unique character, subscribes to 17 databases of its own. A tabulated picture is given below:

Table 6.2 Numbers of Databases in Different University Libraries

Name of the Universities	UGC-Infonet Databases	Self Subscribe Databases	Public Domain Databases
AU	16	0	0
BHU	23	24	—
DU	23	25	41
IGNOU	—	17	52
JMI	21	15	—
JNU	21	15	—
PU	22	—	—
VBU	18	—	—

There are 77 databases in all in these eight universities. But strangely enough only one online database, namely Project Muse, is common to all the universities, and 69 databases are subscribed by single universities. The following Databases are available in seven of the eight university libraries: ACS, AIP, APS, Annual Review, BWP, CUP, IOP, ISID, JCCC, JSTOR, OUP, RSC, SIAM, Springerlink and Taylor and Francis. A tabulated picture is given below:

Table 6.3 Percentage of Availability of Online Database

No. of Database	No. of Universities	% of Occurresnce
1	8	100%
16	7	87%
1	6	75%
3	5	62.5%
4	4	50%
5	3	32.5%
16	2	25%
69	1	12.5%

These are further categorised as:

- Full Text e-Journals - 72
- Bibliographic Databases 15
- E-Books 29
- Total Databases 116

Of these there are 15 bibliographic/indexing databases, while 29 are e-book databases. There is no single common e-book database available in all eight libraries. Among the bibliographic databases, DELNET and ISID are most popular, which are available in seven libraries, while MathSciNet is subscribed by six university libraries. Exemptions are Assam and Viswabharati Universities. It is natural and normal as each central university located in different region has its own requirements based upon its courses of study and areas of research. The subject needs of the JNU differ from that of Delhi University, while Jamia has its own needs. Need and Specialisation of IGNOU are of quite different nature. Still some of the databases are very common to all universities especially the Project Muse, JSTOR, American Chemical Society, American Institute of Physics, American Physical Society, Annual Review, Blackwell Publishing, Cambridge University Press, Institute of Physics, Oxford University of Press, Royal Society of Chemistry, SIAM, Springerlink and Taylor and Francis.

Retrieval Techniques

Net Server and CD-ROM mirror servers are very popular among the universities. The university libraries under study no longer provide CD-ROM services. Multimedia databases are available only in DU and JNU, while all the eight libraries own and provide access to full text and bibliographic databases. For academic libraries the two most important consortia are the UGC-Infonet and Indest. All the libraries have self-subscribed as well as consortia based databases, whereas the DU and JNU have also developed in-house databases. Being traditional and general universities under the preview of the UGC, all are members of the UGC-Infonet, while DU is also member of AICTE Indest consortia.

All the universities use commercial as well as open source databases while DU and JNU have also their home grown databases. Open source databases are also available there, but the study found that only DU, BHU, IGNOU and JNU host important open source online databases on their web sites. Other universities are not able to create this kind of facility for their users merely because the staff of these libraries are not conversant with open access sources on the Internet. Databases can be accessed through login and password, but the misuse of these is a common complaint. Therefore, IP access is more suitable.

Now most of the universities allow online access to databases either through their intranet or directly from the Web. Experienced librarians prefer a campus-wide facility for providing access to databases. AU, IGNOU, Jamia, JNU and Viswabharati allow access from limited and specified terminals within campuses. Assam, IGNOU, Jamia, JNU and Viswa-bharati allow access through campus wide Intranet or Internet with identification and password. Many busy scholars and faculty have less time to visit the library. Therefore, access to online information must be provided on their desktops. This requires campus wide Internet accessibility. Further it was found that AU, BHU, DU, Jamia, JNU, PU and Viswabharati allow IP enabled access while IGNOU databases are password based.

Download Facility

Downloading of the required files is a critical issue. In case of commercial databases it is costly as the host library has to pay per download. But indeed it is an essential facility. It has been found that all the libraries provide downloading of PDF and HTML files, while image downloading facilities are available in all except at BHU and DU. RTF downloading is not permitted by BHU, DU and Jamia Millia Islamia, Whereas word file are not downloadable at BHU, DU and Jamia. DU and JNU provide DBMS software to download the data oriented information.

Data Retrieval Techniques

Some of the universities provide common databases

linked through federated search. Only DU has the federated search engine GIST find. In this survey, only DU and PU revealed their online search techniques while the other libraries kept these confidential. DU uses Boolean, Interactive, and Proximity searches, while PU uses quick search. Simple search Advanced/Boolean search in addition to menudriven searches are provided by their vendors. Both these libraries provide facilities for further refinement of large chunks of search output to make the search more precise and relevant. Nevertheless, none of the universities use data mining.

Complexity of Information Retrieval

Indeed information retrieval techniques vary from university to university system. It depends upon both internal and external factor of database. In the questionnaire about 48 aspects or facilities for information retrieval were identified and the users of these eight libraries were asked to mark their ease of use on the Likert scale as:

- Easy 3
- Challenging 2
- Difficult 1

The mean value of university wise pattern is given below:

Table 6.4 Complexity Level of IR in Different University Libraries

Universities	AU	BHU	DU	IGNOU	JMI	JNU	PU	VBU
Mean	2.58	1.95	2.54	2.52	2.22	2.61	2.37	2.34
Std. Deviation	(0.54)	(0.92)	(2.54)	(0.64)	(0.85)	(0.57)	(0.6)	(0.89)

User Orientation

For optimum use of all resources and services of a library, user orientation programmes, especially of new users, are a proven effective measure. User orientation is the most important component in the online databases for the users to gain knowledge and enhance usability of databases. All the university libraries in this study have positively voted for provision of such programmes to help users in the effective use of the retrieval system for information access. This survey found that orientation programme are conducted by all except AU, BHU, IGNOU, and Viswa Bharati.

It is important to note that regular orientation programmes are required to make the users familiar with new feature of new databases. DU conducted programmes as "How to search the online databases," while the Pondicherry library provides instructions in the use of library resources including eresources and effective online searching. BHU conducts programmes on Science Direct and Proquest. DU provides need-based instruction and PU provides general instruction in effective search and the publishers also conducted such programmes to faciliatets searching of their supplied databases.

DU conducts such programmes throughout the years, while PU organises orientation of the users at the beginning of the academic years. PU also offers need based person to person training. It is clear that there is no uniform pattern of conducting user's orientation programmes. Indeed we need a dedicated library staff for online training of library users, especially in the electronic environment. There are posts of information scientist in universities funded initially by the by UGC.

Those hired are mostly from computer science and not conversant with library philosophy and routine. There is an urgent need of a designated post for an online librarian who can provide assistance in using e-resources and may also take care of any aspect of user orientation for sharing and dissemination of library e-resources. The survey showed that none of the library staff has any formal education and training in online searching. Most have learned it on the job, and most have learned by trial and error.

XML AND RELATIONAL DATABASES: USES AND OPPORTUNITIES FOR LIBRARIES

Extensible Markup Language (XML) is becoming an indispensable tool for virtually every type of content that is digitally produced. The advantages of XML for libraries have been well described by others. On a general level, XML has at least three key advantages:

1. *XML is standard*: XML is a subset of Standard Generalised Markup Language (SGML), a well

established and highly regarded ISO standard. XML also offers mechanisms (document type definitions, and more recently, XML Schema) to encourage and enforce common definitions of the logical structure of a document so that standards for the documents themselves are easier to apply.

2. *XML is extensible*: XML has no limits on the number of markup languages that can be defined using it, and each of these languages can consist of an unlimited number of tags. This flexibility is essential for fostering the widespread adoption of XML and helps explain why XML has been utilised for markup languages in every conceivable subject area, ranging from chess playing to mind reading.
3. *XML is well supported*: It seems that almost every serious Web technology is now expected to define its relationship to XML, and XML has fostered an explosion of related technologies. The W3C has made many tools and toolkits freely available to Web developers, and utilities and applications for XML are being developed by a worldwide community of vendors, open source contributors, and other groups that seek to move information across the Web.

XML has been used extensively for authoring standalone documents, but database solutions for storing and managing large collections of materials in XML format are becoming more common. As Bourett, a researcher who tracks developments in XML databases, points out, choosing between an RDBMS and other database options for storing XML often comes down to whether you are working with data or documents. If the XML content is usually manipulated at the individual field level, needs to be accessed with standard query and reporting tools, and pulls together information from sources that are updated and maintained separately, then a Relational Database Management System (RDBMS) approach may make the most sense.

Examples of this kind of 'data-centric' content include purchase orders, flight schedules, and scientific data. If the

XML content is largely contained in individual documents, and the content will be edited and updated at the document level, then Object Orientated Databases (OODBMS), Object/ Relational Databases, and other solutions that can maintain XML documents as a more complete unit on the backend will be preferred. Data housed in an RDBMS are typically based on individual rows in tables, using 'keys' or 'ids' to pull together content dynamically.

Most RDBMS solutions for storing XML assemble XML representations of the data on the fly. Object relational databases and some RDBMS addons, such as Oracle's Internet File System (IFS), step slightly outside of the standard RDBMS tables to work with Binary Large Object (BLOB) or other mechanisms built into the database to store whole XML documents without parceling pieces of it to separate tables. This allows the document to be stored with all tags and ordering preserved. Of course, the data and document distinction is not absolute, and there are other factors that can influence the choice of a database. An organisation may have built up a high level of Oracle experience, for example, and that would have a huge impact on any data management decisions. Libraries are also in a somewhat unique situation in that they house collections of both data-centric and document-centric materials that may require database solutions.

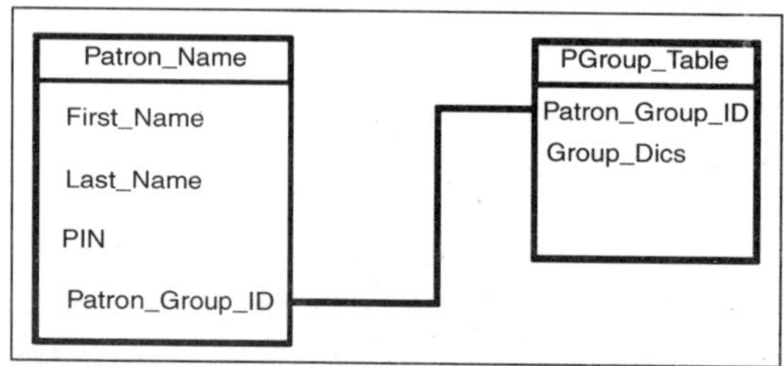

Fig 6.5 The Table with Patron Information (Patron Table) is Linked to another Table (Pgroup Table) Describing the Patron Group

For example, libraries with finding aids in Encoded Archival Description (EAD) format or full text materials marked up with Text Encoding Initiative (TEI) are more likely to favour 'document-centric' solutions and require extensive full text searching capabilities that are more prevalent in OODBMS and Object/ Relational Databases. Libraries are even more likely to deal with content that is 'data-centric', such as purchase orders and circulation records; they may already have RDBMSs in place to support the processing activities associated with this data.

MIDDLEWARE ALTERNATIVES

A number of middleware mapping tools exist for layering XML representations of information that is housed in an RDBMS on top of individual tables, such as IBM's DatabaseDOM. The middleware typically uses Structured Query Language (SQL) to pull together the fields needed for the XML input/output. The advantages of this approach are that this greatly increases the number of database systems that a library can select from because all major RDBMSs support SQL, and that this allows great flexibility for moving from one database to another. For formats like MARC, these tools also offer the possibility of using XML technologies without losing the robustness of relational databases for maintaining content and linkages that are updated by multiple users.

The disadvantages of this approach include the overhead required to assemble and disassemble XML documents as they move in and out of the database, and the extra groundwork to define an XML representation that takes full advantage of both the RDBMS and XML technologies. A good example of an XML mapping tool for relational databases is Castor, an open source project from Exolabs. The mapping file in Castor determines how the XML will be produced from the contents of the RDBMS. In addition to defining whether a field in the RDBMS is to be rendered as a node or an attribute, an ID reference is provided that identifies the records in the appropriate table. Castor is very 'Java-centric,' which can be an advantage or disadvantage depending on how comfortable an organisation is with the Java platform. By working with Java, a developer can use Castor to render the records in an RDBMS accessible and updatable as XML documents. Databases that can be used with Castor include Oracle, MySQL, and PostgreSQL.

THE WEB AS THE WORLD'S BIGGEST RELATIONAL DATABASE

The way that an RDBMS references rows from multiple tables can be compared to Web links. A Web page is, in some ways, much like an RDBMS 'view' of disparate data. From a user perspective, the content is brought together based on a predefined logic and a series of 'keys' or 'pointers' that identify relevant material. A dynamically generated Web page comes even closer to the conceptual model of an RDBMS, particularly if much of the content of the page is based on remote network resources retrieved through URLs. For example, a search of a library catalogue on the Web typically involves a cgi-bin programme that dynamically displays results using HTML. Each result record is usually linked to a fuller display via a URL that specifies from where the information is to be retrieved.

The linking mechanisms of the Web have recently been leveraged to support the OpenURL framework. The OpenURL framework has been proposed as an architecture for retrieving references to scholarly works by enabling third parties to provide links for a referenced item. Although OpenURLs have typically been deployed to provide links to the full text of scholarly works, the framework can also be utilised to identify a catalogued item in an ILS. Ex Libris' ALEPH500 System, for example, directly supports OpenURL, and exploratory work has been carried out to generalise the OpenURL framework beyond reference linking scholarly environments.

If the Web can be thought of as an ever-growing RDBMS, and OpenURLs can be utilised to provide 'RDBMS-like' standard and precise links between specific items in information systems, then there are possibilities for providing extensive distributed search and retrieval functions in Web-based library services. For example, a remote database consisting of Library of Congress names and subject headings could be searched within a browser environment, and the results could provide links to items in the local catalogue.

Web-based union catalogues support standardised indexing and searching at a central location. With OpenURLs, links can be made to point to holdings and other localised information within the member library's Integrated Library System.

All of this fits within the RDBMS notion of creating and maintaining data with as little duplication as possible, and linking it together to provide a logical view of the content itself. XML plays a role by greatly enhancing the linking mechanisms of the Web. XML technologies such as Xinclude, Xpath, and Xlink, provide sophisticated methods for drawing on network resources. Xinclude allows the contents of a separate XML resource to be inserted into an XML document based on a link. Xpath will be familiar to anyone who has worked with XSTL and other XML stylesheet tools.

It allows the creation of expressions for specifying every visual and interface portion of a document. Xlink is the XML linking language and offers much more sophisticated types of linking than currently offered by the familiar HREF and NAME elements found in HTML. Xlink's extended element can name one or more linked resources. The arc element in this example tells an application about the behaviour expected when moving through the linked resources. The role and title attributes are used to describe the function of the linked resource in the context of the local resource. Role is meant to be descriptive to the application and title is meant to be descriptive to the user. In this case, the roles are meant to identify an author's works and biographies. The *acutate* element describes how the resources should appear. The value 'onRequest' specifies that the resource should appear when the link is selected, and the value 'embed' for the *show* attribute tells the application to insert the specified resource inline within the current document.

Finally, an *item* element is used to represent where this particular resource can be found in physical form in the library. If an XML representation of an RDBMS-based library catalogue or other library database is made available, the library can make use of XML linking technologies and other XML tools for manipulating database contents. OpenURL lays the groundwork for using links as virtual keys to content that goes far beyond individual tables, and the content can be as broad as the diversity of the Web itself.

STANDARDS FOR CREATING BIBLIOGRAPHIC DATABASES

The concept of "standard" in the field of library and information science is interpreted as codes of cataloguing rules, classification schemes, subject headings and various other documents contained recommendations for good library practice, all of which are subject to varying interpretation. But, for another professionals, standards are extremely precise technical specifications for communication between software and machines in an automated information-processing environment.

For example, Operating Systems, TCP/IP, etc. Standards are documented agreements containing technical specifications or other precise criteria to be used consistently as rules, guidelines, or definitions of characteristics, to ensure that materials, products, processes and services are fit for their purpose Field of bibliographic standards are not limited to the rules only but spread up to the authority files such as person names, corporate names, subject headings, classification schemes, series names, institution names, software and standardisation form and format, etc. In beginning, during the initiation of automation to library professionals, there was not much focus on bibliographic standards and were creating databases in any formats. That affected to the automation of their libraries, which forced them to think over the issue. Now, gradually, the libraries and information centres are realising the importance of bibliographic standards.

Centres like Information and Library Network (INFLIBNET), Ahmedabad is playing important role in bringing all libraries together to work on a single platform of standards with linking under one huge national network, *i.e.*, UGC-Infonet. INFLIBNET Centre is an Inter-University Centre of University Grants Commission (UGC), working on Academic library system in India. In 1990, UGC launched it as a programme for five years on pilot basis.

On June 1996, the programme was recognised as a full-fledged Centre. To know more about the Centre. UGC-Infonet is a project of UGC being implemented by INFLIBNET Centre in collaboration with ERNET (Education and Research

Network), New Delhi. It is an Intra-Network of Indian universities and colleges across the country based on the Open IP platform, employing state-of-the-art technologies like IP or TV, enabling online response to queries. The network facilitates Intranet and Internet access to its users on high data rates.

STANDARDS FOR BIBLIOGRAPHIC DATABASE

Well-known simple definition of database is a set of records and record is a set of fields, where, field is a combination of different pieces of information. Bibliographic database is a database of resources available at libraries in print format. With the revolution of information technology in the field of libraries, bibliographic catalogue has come up into the form of bibliographic database.

For making compatible with these changes, there, many library institutions have come up with different standards and formats such as CCF, AUSMARC, CANMARC, UKMARC, USMARC, UNIMARC, MARC21, AACR2, ISBD, LCSH, MeSH, etc. Some of the Internationally recognised standards and formats being used by many libraries of different countries for creating databases. As per the INFLIBNET's guidelines following standards are recommended for use:

Standardised Bibliographic Formats

During the inception of the Programme, The Task Group on "Union Catalogue, Data Capturing and Standardisation" was constituted by UGC. The Task Group was assisted by a Sub-Committee on implementation of Common Communication Format (CCF) for data capturing and data exchange. Later on, the Sub-Committee formalised some fields based on CCF and named it as "Guidelines for Data Capturing: a user manual". During the initial stage of automation, Micro CDS/ISIS software (developed by Unesco) were suggested to use for creating bibliographic databases based on the format recommended by the Centre.

Simultaneously, other DBMS such as DBase, FoxPro, FoxBase, etc., were also being used by different libraries for creating the databases. In addition, the Centre had also the library house keeping software called "ILMS – Integrated Library Management System" developed on COBOL language on Unix platform, and was distributed freely to the member libraries of the Centre. Later in February 2000, Centre developed another library house keeping software called "SOUL – Software for University Libraries" on Power Builder language on Windows platform by using the client-server architecture to keep in mind the shortcomings being faced in ILMS software.

The software is developed based on the format formalised by Sub-Committee of the Task Force. Later, early 2001, The Ministry of Human Resource Development (MHRD), Govt. of India visualises building up a national database of library holdings in the country based on the MARC21 format. Further, after approval the committee directed INFLIBNET Centre to implement the MARC21 format in all libraries of the country. In this regards, the Centre formed the MARC21 Core Group during December 2001, which formalised the fields for implementing it with the SOUL library house keeping software.

The main reason for preferring MARC21 over CCF and other formats was that most of the countries in the world use MARC and it is comprehensive having number of fields. Also there is constant development taking place in MARC21 and is updated regularly whereas CCF has become stagnant. In the first meeting MARC21 Core Group were come out with the following results

- MARC21 Code list for field identification. Available on following web site:
- http://web.inflibnet.ac.in/info/dwldmarc21_codelist.pdf
- Field list for Name and Subject Authority Database. Accessible through:
- http://web.inflibnet.ac.in/info/dwld/auth_tag_lst.pdf
- Fields for the Indian Manuscript Database. Available at:
- http://web.inflibnet.ac.in/info/dwld/finalmanuscript.pdf

STANDARD FOR RENDERING INFORMATION/ BIBLIOGRAPHIC DESCRIPTIONS

AACR2R, ISBD and CCC are standards for bibliographic descriptions. But, INFLIBNET Centre suggests their participating libraries to follow the Anglo American Cataloging Rules-II (AACRII) Revised version for rendering bibliographic information.

STANDARDISED SUBJECT HEADINGS

Different subject headings list are available, developed by different institutions such as LCSH, Sear's List of Subject Headings, MeSH, Thesaurus, etc. But INFLIBNET suggests to its member library to use LCSH (for generalised subject headings) and Engineering Index, MeSH and thesaurus (for specialised Subject Headings).

STANDARD FOR CLASSIFICATION SCHEMES

There are various classification schemes have been developed by different organisations for classifying the books on different subjects. Functionally, most of the libraries are using the Dewey Decimal Classification (DDC) for assigning the Classification Number to the documents. But, under INFLIBNET umbrella, all the libraries are free to use any classification scheme for classifying the document, as it is very difficult for any library to reclassify the entire collection based on any new scheme. As per the library practice any classification scheme can be used as MARC21 has capability to adopt any kind of classification schemes.

ISO–2709 INFORMATION EXCHANGE FORMAT

This standard specifies the requirements for generalised interchange format that will accommodate data describing all forms of material. It describes a generalised structure designed specifically for exchange of data between processing systems and not necessarily for use as a processing format within systems.

The format may be used for the interchange of records using various communication media. INFLIBNET Centre recommends to follow this Exchange Format for contributing records to the Centre. The exchange format has implemented too with the in-house developed software SOUL for exchanging records. Physical structure of the implemented information exchange format is given below.

Physical Structure

General Structure of the Record:

Leader	Directory	Data Fields	R/S
R/S =Record Separator			

Leader

Each record begins with a leader of fixed length of 24 character positions and is the first instance of the ISO 2709 format of a record. It contains:

- *Record length (5 characters):* The length of the record includes the leader, directory, data fields and record separator.
- *Record Status Code (1 character):* Always '0' for output files, ignored on input files.
- *Implementation Codes (4 characters):* These codes are defined for each specific implementation of the ISO 2709 format. Second character position represents Bibliographic level codes (*i.e.,* s- serials, m- single volume monographs, c- multivolume monographs, a- component part) and rest of the character positioned not used. Here, Bibliographic level is defined here as per the INFLIBNET's use. For the MARC21 based records, it follows the description defined for bibliographic level in MARC21 bibliographic format.
- *Indicator length (1 character):* This is always '0', because here at INFLIBNET database indicator is not being used. But the value is '2', when we export records from SOUL to MARC21 in ISO 2709 format.
- *Subfield identifier length (1 character):* '2' The subfield identifier length. This shows the number of characters being used for the subfield identifier.
- *Base address of data (5 characters):* A decimal number

indicating the number of control characters (length of leader plus directory and field separator) which precede the variable data fields. This number, when added to the starting address of the record, gives the address of the first character of the variable fields.

- *For user systems (3 characters):* These character positions are not used. Always '000' in output files.
- *Length of "Length of Datafield" field (1 character):* '4' the length of "Length of Datafield" in the directory. (Use of 4 characters permits datafields as long as 9,999 characters)
- *Length of "Starting character" position (1 character):* '5' the length is "Starting character position" in the directory.
- *Rest (2 characters):* These character positions are not used. Always sets on '00'.

Directory

A directory entry in this bibliographic record is made up of a tag, length-of-field, and field starting position. It is of variable length and consists of a series of fixed fields, referred to as "entries". One directory entry is associated with each datafield present in the record. Each directory entry is 12 characters in length and is divided into three parts:

- *Tag:* A three numeric ASCII character code identifying the datafield, which corresponds to the directory entry. In software, names of the fields are being used in alphabetical name, but during the export in ISO 2709 format and display on screen, it converts in three-numeric digit ASCII character code.
- *Length of datafield:* A four digit number showing how many characters are occupied by the datafield, including datafield separator but excluding the record separator code if the datafield is the last field in the record.
- *Starting character position:* A five-digit number giving the position of the first character of the datafield relative to the base address of data, *i.e.,* the first character of the first of the datafields.

TAG	Field Length	Starting Character Position

Datafields

A datafield consists of subfield and datafield separator:

- *Subflield:* A subfield consists of a subfield identifier followed by a data string, which is terminated by either another subfield identifier or a field separator. A subfield identifier consists of a subfield identifier flag, *i.e.,* cap (^) sign followed by one another character, that can be alphabet a to z (small or capital) and numeric 1 to 9, INFLIBNET Centre uses here small alphabets. For MARC21 based records "$" graphical sign is used as a subfield identifier.
- *Datafield Separator:* The datafield separator, *i.e.,* hash (#) sign constitutes the final character of every datafield. ASCII value 30 (character 1/14 of ISO 646) is being used as a field separator in MARC21 based data.

A datafield, which has a single subfield, will be organised as follows:

Subfield Identifier 2 Character	Subfield Variable	Field Sepatator 1 Characters

A Datafield,which has two Subfields will be Organised as follows:

First Subfield Identifier 2 Characters	First Subfield Variable	Second Subfield Identifier 2 Characters	Second Subfield Variable	Field Seperator 1 Character

Record Terminator/ Separator

The record terminator is the final character of the record, *i.e.,* hash (#) sign. It follows the field separator of the final datafield of the record. ASCII 29 (character 1/13 of ISO 646) is being used as record separator in MARC21 based data.

OTHER STANDARDS RELATED TO BIBLIOGRAPHIC DATABASE

There are some other standards related to the bibliographic databases.

Z39.50 Retrieval Protocol

Z39.50 refers to the International Standard, ISO 23950: "Information Retrieval (Z39.50): Application Service Definition and Protocol Specification", and to ANSI/NISO Z39.50. The standard specifies a client/serverbased protocol for searching and retrieving information from remote databases.

OAI (Open Archive Initiative)

The Open Archive Initiative (OAI) for metadata harvesting is a new protocol dedicated to solving problems of digital library interoperability by defining simple protocols, most recently for the exchange of metadata. Although, Z39.50 Information Retrieval Protocol is also one of the harvesting protocols. Some digital library systems are using for retrieving and searching the records for example Maxwell System. It is crucial to explain, discuss, and disambiguate the concepts and terminology used among OAI implementers to harvesting approach to interoperability. The harvesting protocol defined by the OAI is a request/ response protocol with 6 request types, *viz. Identity, ListMetadataFormats, ListSets, GetRecords ListRecord, and ListIdentifiers.* It has defined in such a way to support a common set of principles and a technical framework to achieve interoperability. Although, both the standards are not being used with the INFLIBNET database right now, but being explored to implement it in near future.

PURPOSE OF THE BIBLIOGRAPHIC STANDARDS

Mostly, purpose of using these standards for creating bibliographic databases or suggesting using it at libraries of India, has following reasons behind it:

- Pursuing Universal Bibliographic Control
- Exchange of information among union databases for the purpose of global resource sharing
- Cooperation at the local level, transferring data from one system to another

IMPORTANCE OF THE BIBLIOGRAPHIC STANDARDS

Following bibliographic standards for creating the databases produces following importance:

- It makes uniformity in records

- It provides better resource sharing between different resource centres
- It helps in exchanging of records and facilitates it without data loss
- It helps in creating national/ International bibliographic union database
- It helps to adopt any system and provides platform interoperability

CONCLUSION

Now a days, libraries are using web technology extensively for user services to provide dynamic services to the remote users. Web technology currently available is helping the libraries to achieve their purposes. Although, web technology available, especially from Microsoft, is easier to setup the applications. It requires less programming skill and, is suitable for librarians. However, there is a need for librarians to get extensive exposure with the computer and communications technology in general and web technology specifically. The advancement in database technology especially RDBMS has made them ideal for library applications. These RDBMS provide simple architecture, easy to design and are equipped with flexible data exchange interface and, thus, present ideal solutions for web-enabled databases in libraries.

7

Web Browser

A web browser (commonly referred to as a browser) is a software application for retrieving, presenting and traversing information resources on the World Wide Web. An *information resource* is identified by a Uniform Resource Identifier (URI) and may be a web page, image, video or other piece of content. Hyperlinks present in resources enable users easily to navigate their browsers to related resources. A web browser can also be defined as an application software or program designed to enable users to access, retrieve and view documents and other resources on the Internet.

Although browsers are primarily intended to use the World Wide Web, they can also be used to access information provided by web servers in private networks or files in file systems. The major web browsers are Chrome, Firefox, Internet Explorer, Opera, and Safari.

The first web browser was invented in 1990 by Sir Tim Berners-Lee. It was called WorldWideWeb (no spaces) and was later renamed Nexus.

In 1993, browser software was further innovated by Marc Andreessen with the release of Mosaic (later Netscape), "the world's first popular browser", which made the World Wide Web system easy to use and more accessible to the average person. Andreesen's browser sparked the internet boom of the 1990s. The introduction of Mosaic in 1993 – one of the first graphical web browsers – led to an explosion in web use. Andreessen, the leader of the Mosaic team at NCSA, soon started his own company, named Netscape, and released the Mosaic-influenced Netscape Navigator in 1994, which quickly became the world's most popular browser, accounting for 90% of all web use at its peak.

Microsoft responded with its Internet Explorer in 1995, also heavily influenced by Mosaic, initiating the industry's first browser war. Bundled with Windows, Internet Explorer gained dominance in the web browser market; Internet Explorer usage share peaked at over 95% by 2002.

Opera debuted in 1996; although it has never achieved widespread use, having less than 2% browser usage share as of February 2012 according to Net Applications. Its Opera-mini version has an additive share, in April 2011 amounting to 1.1% of overall browser use, but focused on the fast-growing mobile phone web browser market, being preinstalled on over 40 million phones. It is also available on several other embedded systems, including Nintendo's Wii video game console.

In 1998, Netscape launched what was to become the Mozilla Foundation in an attempt to produce a competitive browser using the open source software model. That browser would eventually evolve into Firefox, which developed a respectable following while still in the beta stage of development; shortly after the release of Firefox 1.0 in late 2004, Firefox (all versions) accounted for 7% of browser use. As of August 2011, Firefox has a 28% usage share.

Apple's Safari had its first beta release in January 2003; as of April 2011, it had a dominant share of Apple-based web browsing, accounting for just over 7% of the entire browser market.

The most recent major entrant to the browser market is Chrome, first released in September 2008. Chrome's take-up has increased significantly year on year, by doubling its usage share from 8% to 16% by August 2011. This increase seems largely to be at the expense of Internet Explorer, whose share has tended to decrease from month to month. In December 2011, Chrome overtook Internet Explorer 8 as the most widely used web browser but still has lower usage than all versions of Internet Explorer combined.

FUNCTION

The primary purpose of a web browser is to bring

information resources to the user ("retrieval" or "fetching"), allow them to view the information ("display", "rendering"), and then access other information ("navigation", "following links").

This process begins when the user inputs a Uniform Resource Locator (URL), for example *http://en.wikipedia.org/*, into the browser. The prefix of the URL, the Uniform Resource Identifier or URI, determines how the URL will be interpreted. The most commonly used kind of URI starts with *http:* and identifies a resource to be Retrieved over the Hypertext Transfer Protocol (HTTP). Many browsers also support a variety of other prefixes, such as *https:* for HTTPS, *ftp:* for the File Transfer Protocol, and *file:* for local files. Prefixes that the web browser cannot directly handle are often handed off to another application entirely. For example, *mailto:* URIs are usually passed to the user's default e-mail application, and *news:* URIs are passed to the user's default newsgroup reader.

In the case of *http*, *https*, *file*, and others, once the resource has been Retrieved the web browser will display it. HTML and associated content (image files, formatting information such as CSS, etc.) is passed to the browser's layout engine to be transformed from markup to an interactive document, a process known as "rendering". Aside from HTML, web browsers can generally display any kind of content that can be part of a web page. Most browsers can display images, audio, video, and XML files, and often have plug-ins to support Flash applications and Java applets. Upon encountering a file of an unsupported type or a file that is set up to be downloaded rather than displayed, the browser prompts the user to save the file to disk.

Information resources may contain hyperlinks to other information resources. Each link contains the URI of a resource to go to. When a link is clicked, the browser navigates to the resource indicated by the link's target URI, and the process of bringing content to the user begins again.

FEATURES

Available web browsers range in features from minimal,

text-based user interfaces with bare-bones support for HTML to rich user interfaces supporting a wide variety of file formats and protocols. Browsers which include additional components to support e-mail, Usenet news, and Internet Relay Chat (IRC), are sometimes referred to as "Internet suites" rather than merely "web browsers".

All major web browsers allow the user to open multiple information resources at the same time, either in different browser windows or in different tabs of the same window. Major browsers also include pop-up blockers to prevent unwanted windows from "popping up" without the user's consent.

Most web browsers can display a list of web pages that the user has *bookmarked* so that the user can quickly return to them. Bookmarks are also called "Favorites" in Internet Explorer. In addition, all major web browsers have some form of built-in web feed aggregator. In Firefox, web feeds are formatted as "live bookmarks" and behave like a folder of bookmarks corresponding to recent entries in the feed. In Opera, a more traditional feed reader is included which stores and displays the contents of the feed.

Furthermore, most browsers can be extended via plug-ins, downloadable components that provide additional features.

User Interface

Most major web browsers have these user interface elements in common:

- *Back* and *forward* buttons to go back to the previous resource and forward respectively.
- A *refresh* or *reload* button to reload the current resource.
- A *stop* button to cancel loading the resource. In some browsers, the stop button is merged with the reload button.
- A *home* button to return to the user's home page.
- An address bar to input the Uniform Resource Identifier (URI) of the desired resource and display it.

- A search bar to input terms into a search engine. In some browsers, the search bar is merged with the address bar.
- A status bar to display progress in loading the resource and also the URI of links when the cursor hovers over them, and page zooming capability.

Major browsers also possess incremental find features to search within a web page.

PRIVACY AND SECURITY

Most browsers support HTTP Secure and offer quick and easy ways to delete the web cache, cookies, and browsing history. For a comparison of the current security vulnerabilities of browsers, see comparison of web browsers.

Standards Support

Early web browsers supported only a very simple version of HTML. The rapid development of proprietary web browsers led to the development of non-standard dialects of HTML, leading to problems with interoperability. Modern web browsers support a combination of standards-based and *de facto* HTML and XHTML, which should be rendered in the same way by all browsers.

Extensibility

A browser extension is a computer program that extends the functionality of a web browser. Every major web browser supports the development of browser extensions.

TYPES OF WEB BROWSERS

All web browsers are application programs that are developed to access information on World Wide Web. Although the primary application of all the web browsers is the same, they differ from each other in more than one aspect. The distinguishing areas are:

- Platform: Linux, Windows, Mac, BSD and other Unix
- Protocols: FTP, SFTP, SAMBA, HTTP, IMAP, etc.
- Graphical User Interface (GUI)

- Layout Engine: Amaya, Gecko, Trident, KHTML, WebKit
- Mobile Compatibility
- HTML5 Support
- Open Source
- Proprietary

However, the general, primary and secondary features and facilities offered by web browsers include downloads, bookmarks, and password management. They also offer functions like spell checking, search engine toolbars, tabbed browsing, advertisement filtering, HTML access keys and pop-up blocking.

INTERNET EXPLORER

It was developed by Microsoft in 1994 and released in 1995 as a supportive package to Microsoft Windows line of operating systems. According to statistics, its usage share from 1999 to 2003-04 was around 95%. Microsoft occasionally releases updates for the previous versions of IE, which have some enhanced capabilities. IE has come up a preview release of Internet Explorer 10. The 'favicon', which is the short form of *favorite icon,* was introduced first in IE, and was later adopted by many other browsers. Initially, IE did not support tabbed browsing. But today, it can be used even in the older versions, by installing toolbars.

Features: There are regular Microsoft updates that IE supports. Favicon allows an image to be used as a bookmark. It supports Integrated Windows Authentication.

MOZILLA FIREFOX

It is owned by Mozilla Corporation and was the result of an experimentation. 'Mozilla Firefox' was officially announced in February 2004. It was earlier named Phoenix, Firebird, and eventually Firefox. It is the second-most famous browser after Internet Explorer, as there were around 100 million downloads within a year of its release. Until November 2008, 700 million downloads were recorded. Since the release of Firefox, the sale of Internet Explorer has gone down drastically. It has around

22% of the market share at present. It has undergone many updates and version changes that were made to improve usability to the universal users.

Features: As it is an open source software, it allows everyone to access the code. It supports tabbed browsing that allows the user to open multiple sites in a single window. Session storage is also an important feature of Firefox, which allows the user to regain access to the open tabs after he has closed the browser window.

SAFARI

This is a web browser from Apple Inc., which is compatible with Mac OS X, Microsoft Windows, and the iPhone OS. Safari was released by Apple in January 2003 as a public beta. If you need to fill an online form with your personal information, AutoFill is a feature that automatically does that for you, with the help of information that is stored in your address book or Outlook.

Features: The Safari 4 beta had many features like VoiceOver screen reader, that reads aloud everything that is on the screen, including text and web links. It also has features like CSS Canvas, LiveConnect, XML 1.0, and JavaScript support, and Cover Flow. 'Grammar Checking' is an interesting built-in feature, which performs a grammar check on the typed text and gives suggestions to correct your sentence if wrong. Also, there is a resizable web search box option available.

OPERA

This browser was developed by Opera Software in 1996. It is a well-known browser that is mainly used in Internet-activated mobile phones, PDAs, and smartphones. Opera Mini and Opera Mobile are the browsers used in smartphones. It is compatible with many operating systems such as Solaris, Linux, Mac OS X, and Microsoft Windows. It is also compatible with Symbian and Windows Mobile operating systems for smartphones and PDAs. The company claims that Opera is the fastest browser in the world.

Features: It also has some common functions like zoom and fit-to-width, content blocking, tabs and sessions, download manager with BitTorrent, and mouse gestures.

GOOGLE CHROME

This web browser was developed by Google. Its beta and commercial versions were released in September 2008 for Microsoft Windows. The browser versions for Mac OS X are under development. The browser options are very similar to that of Safari, the settings locations are similar to Internet Explorer 7, and the window design is based on Windows Vista.

Features: The main standout feature is the malware and phishing warning that the browser suggests when the user wants to browse a site. Also, there is a user tracking option available with Chrome.

NETSCAPE NAVIGATOR

It was developed by Netscape Communications Corporation and was most popular in the 1990s. Exceptional features were provided at the time of its release, which helped it to rise to fame with a market share of more than 50% in the 1990s. It was compatible with almost every operating system. Since 2002, it has almost disappeared from the market due to strong competition from rivals like Internet Explorer, Mozilla Firefox, Safari, etc. It had undergone many version changes to maintain its stake in the market, none of which were very successful.

Features: Netscape Messenger is an email and news client for Netscape Navigator 9. Also, another feature is Netscape Publishing System that allows commercial sites to publish articles and charge users for accessing them.

LYNX

It was initially developed by Distributed Computing Group at University of Kansas only for using in the campus. However, with the addition of new protocols, the new version was launched on the Internet in 1992. A cross-platform browser that runs on Unix, VMS, DOS, Microsoft Windows, Mac Os, OS/2 and others. Lynx is a text based browser.

Features: Though being the oldest amongst the current lot of web browsers, it can be remotely accessed over Telnet and SSH. This feature enables Lynx to be used for testing a website's performance from any geographical location.

It has a wide base of visually impaired users due to "braille terminal" and "text-to-speech" interface.

OMNIWEB

It was developed by The Omni Group and released in the year 1995. The browser is exclusively available for Apple's Mac OS X 10.4.8 or later versions, and it is a freeware. The latest version that is in the market is 5.5 that has a customized WebKit and a FTP folder display options.

Features: One of the features that this browser offers is the creation of Workspaces where one can store the personal browser history. It even gives freedom to share the same with other Omni users. The ad blocking feature even blocks images from the restricted sites.

VOYAGER

It is a web browser that is developed by VaporWare for Amiga computers. Its stable release was in the year 2000. It operates on AmigaOS and MorphOS.

Features: HTML 3.2, HTML 4, SSL, Flash and many other features are supported by this browser.

KONQUEROR

It is a KHTML based engine that was developed by KDE and initially released in 1996. It supports protocols like FTP, SFTP, SAMBA, HTTP, IMAP and others.

Features: The browser customizes the search and the user can get the website related data by just typing the keywords. The passwords and usernames are automatically stored in the Kwallet for future use. It will block all the ads and pop-ups, automatically!

ICAB

It is developed by Alexander Clauss and its initial release

was in the year 1999. The web browser is actively developed for 68k-based Macintoshes. The operating system that it works on is the Mac OS X.

Features: The features of the web browser include the filter manager. The user can filter the advertisements and videos; these can be easily blocked. There is a HTML validity checker that gives an error report if there are any issues with the HTML codes. The browser also has multiple language support. If there are any updates available for the sites that are bookmarked, the browser automatically updates the same.

WEB

This browser was originally called "Epiphany" till its 3.4th version, which was released in March, 2012. The initial release was in the year 2003. It is specifically developed for the GNOME desktop by The GNOME Web Browser Developers. It supports Linux, BSD and Mac OS X. The browser is WebKit based and supports a part of HTML5 plus XHTML.

Features: There are a few extensions that come with the browser like Ad Blocker, Gestures (performs actions by mouse gestures) and many more.

MAXTHON

It is developed by Maxthon International Limited for Microsoft Windows, Mac OS X and iOS along with Android for Maxthon mobiles. The browser is recently upgraded for 10 inch tablets in 2011. The latest Maxthon 3 version supports WebKit and Trident web engines.

Features: Its features include Ad Hunter (block ads, pop-ups), Adobe Flash and ActiveX blocker, customizable skins, partial GECKO support and many more.

CAMINO

Launched under the "The Camino Project" at Apple Inc., Camino's initial launch was in 2002. It is an open source and free web browser; specifically designed for Mac OS X. It is multilingual and supports HTML5. The browser is based on Gecko layout engine.

Features: Like any browser, this too supports ad and pop-up blocker. The standout feature from the other Mac based browsers is the Cocoa API which is a proprietary of Apple.

AVANT BROWSER

It is developed by Avant Force with the initial launch in 2004. Avant is a free browser for Windows (2000, XP, 7, Vista). The browser can supports Gecko and WebKit based layout engines. The user is free to choose the layout engine of his choice.

Features: It is available in 41 languages and includes features like full screen mode, automatic page refresh, 21 skin options available, unwanted content blocking and many more.

NETSURF

Netsurf is developed by "The NetSurf Developers" with its stable release in 2012. It has its own layout engine and is built for AmigaOS, Atari OS, Mac OS X, RISC OS, Unix-like platforms and a few third party ports as well.

XOMBRERO

It was originally called xxxterm and developed by Marco Peereboom. The browser's original launch was in May 2012 and the stable release was in September 2012. It is a WebKit based engine with no ad-blocking feature. It supports Windows and Unix-like systems.

A few browsers that were developed a few years ago have been discontinued due to many factors. Here's a list of such browsers.

- *Mosaic:* It is known as the first graphical web browser and was developed by National Center for Supercomputing Applications (NCSA) in 1993. It was used for protocols like FTP, NNTP and Gopher and the platforms where it could be used were Windows, Unix and Amiga. It was later discontinued in 1997.
- *Cello:* It was the first web browser for Microsoft Windows that was developed by Legal Information Institute at Cornell Law School in 1993. The browser was later discontinued in 1994.

- *Arena:* Authored by Dave Raggett in C language, Arena was released in 1995 for Unix. It supported HTML3; HTTP, PNG, JPG, FTP, NNTP, Gopher and others. However, it was later discontinued in 1998.
- *IBM WebExplorer:* IT was developed by IBM in 1995. The operating system that it supported was OS/2. The browser supported HTML 3.0, GIF, etc.
- *SlipKnot:* It was developed by MicroMind, Inc. in the year 1994 for Microsoft Windows. The code was written in C. The browser was named so, because it did not need a SLIP or TCP/IP connection to view graphical content. In June, 2000, MicroMind Inc. homepage declared that SlipKnot was no longer supported by them.
- *iBrowse:* Initially released in 1996, it was the browser for Amico Computer. It supports HTML4, JAVA and SSL. It is a MUI (can generate GUI) based browser. However, since 2007, it is not available for purchase.
- *Agora:* Developed by World Wide Web Consortium, it was an email based browser. For people to use the browser, it had to be first downloaded in the server and then the URL had to be sent to Agora for confirmation. The browser would confirm the request with an approved link via email. It was discontinued in 1997.
- *Oracle PowerBrowser:* This was developed by Oracle Corporation in the year 1996. The browser had the feature that allowed users to host web pages on their own computers. It was, however, discontinued later on.
- *Galeon:* This web browser was released in the year 2000 and was developed by Marco Pesenti Gritti. Galeon was a Gecko (layout engine) based browser and it incorporated a lot of Gecko's features like customizable toolbars, page zooming, etc. Developed for Unix-like operating systems, the browser was discontinued in 2008.
- *Shiira:* This browser was initially released in 2004

for Mac OS X operating system. It was a WebKit based browser and the main goal of its launch was to create a browser that was better than Safari. It was discontinued in 2009.

Over the years, there are a few browsers that are developed to browse specific sites. They are:

Browser	**Used for**
Gollum Browser	Wikipedia
Image Explorer	View, edit images
Flock	Social networking sites

Although there are many web browsers available and many more are likely to arrive in future, only those which are truly exciting and user-friendly will be able to survive market competition and hold on to a substantial market share.

Current Web browsers provide a limited support to personalize the Web, namely bookmarks. In two recent surveys, users report that the use of bookmarks is among the three main problems they have when using the Internet. We see several problems when using bookmarks :

- The number of bookmarks grows linearly with time and it becomes a real challenge for many users to organize this amount of data
- By storing the document URL and title, bookmarks are not representative enough to facilitate information access
- Bookmarks become obsolete when the document URLs change, and the information stored is of little help for users to understand what the page was about and why it was stored
- Although a description field is available, bookmarks do not help users to remember what was interesting in a document and what they thought about it
- Bookmarks do not store the context of the document, giving users no information about how they found it.

As a result, the users are lost in their own information space when they use current bookmark programs. Our approach is to use a Web annotation tool so that users can personalize the documents they read. Current bookmarks can be thought as annotations applying to the entire document. On the other hand, an annotation can identify a specific text in a document and contain additional attributes. The annotation tool thus complements current bookmarks. We see several advantages with an annotation tool:

- Annotations first reduce the cognitive overload imposed to the users when they retrieve a document previously annotated (Marshall, 1998). With the annotations, the users have indices to understand what was important in the document. The navigation inside the document is much easier
- The highlighted texts can be used to augment the document representation. Our studies show that the concatenation of the highlighted texts are helpful to understand the topic of a document
- Even if a document URL is broken, users still have access to the highlighted texts, helping them to recall why it was interesting and was bookmarked
- If the annotation system stores the parent URL of each annotated document, the user is provided with a minimal information about where the document came from.

But beyond these direct applications of the annotation tool, our results also suggest three ways of using the annotations in information retrieval:

- The highlighted texts can be used to build personalized document summaries, thus improving document access and retrieval;
- Automatic document clustering can also use them to generate user-directed document clusters;
- Automatic document classifiers can take advantage of the highlighted text to extract significant words from the documents without using the usual word frequency and inverse document frequency measures.

In the next section, we first review existing annotation tools and discuss why they are not well suited to construct a personal information space where speed and privacy become important issues. We present the traditional approach used in these systems and show how the Document Object Model Level 2 and the new Application Program Interfaces (API) provided by commercial Web browsers will change the architecture of future annotation systems. We present the implementation of our annotation system which uses these new technologies. We then present several experiments showing how the annotations can be used to improve document access and document clustering. We finally discuss the future works including document classification and summarization, and present related works.

WEB ANNOTATION SYSTEMS

The architecture of Web annotation systems has been reviewed in (Vasudevan, 1999). The authors pointed out that new technologies like the Document Object Model (DOM) level 2 will be needed to design good annotation systems. Although the specifications of the DOM Level 2 are not released yet, a popular Web browser implements some of the current recommendations and many new exciting applications are already using it to enhance the browsing experience of Internet users. Instead of describing in details how Web annotation systems used to work, we focus on their weaknesses and detail how the new DOM Level 2 specifications can be used to design new annotation systems. We then discuss the new challenges that should be addressed by future annotation systems.

The Limits of Current Web Annotation Systems

An annotation system usually consists of three modules : the first is used to view existing annotations, the second to create new annotations and the third to store the annotations. An annotation is made of two parts : an *anchor* which is used to locate the annotation in the document, and the *attributes* which include for instance a free comment and the author's name. We are interested here by *inline annotation* systems, meaning that the annotations are attached to a specific text in the document. We will call this text the *highlighted text*.

To implement the first module, annotation systems use an intermediary which resides between the browser and the Internet. Its role is to attach the annotations to the documents requested by the browser before they are displayed. As most Web browsers can be configured to use a proxy, the intermediary has often been implemented in the form of a proxy. Technically, the proxy requires little browser configuration for the user. But a proxy-based intermediary has several limits. Firstly, proxies are not contacted when a local document is loaded in the browser, and local documents cannot be annotated. Secondly, the proxy needs to parse each document and modify its original content to insert annotations. To our knowledge, there is no annotation system designed to parse scripts embedded in Web pages. These scripts are sometimes used to generate the content of a document. But more important, the parsing procedures will need to cope with new Web standards like XML.

Another problem with proxy-based intermediaries is privacy. Since the proxy seats between the browser and the Internet, it can spy every requested URL. Users should be able to turn off the annotation system anytime. Removing the proxy by reconfiguring the browser is possible, but the procedure is tedious and it is likely that most users will not use it. An original approach has been found in CritLink (Yee, 1998) where the proxy is called a mediator. With CritLink, no browser configuration is needed and most of the existing Web browsers can use the annotation tool. The system is simply used by prefixing the URL with http://crit.org. For instance, to see the annotated version of http://www.yahoo.com, one simply change the location to http://crit.org/http://www.yahoo.com. When the CritLink server is contacted, 1) it retrieves the requested document from the internet, 2) adds the annotations attached to it and 3) modifies all the links by prefixing them with http://crit.org. This last step ensures that all subsequent requests will first be forwarded to the CritLink server. To turn off the annotation system, the user only needs to remove the http://crit.org/ prefix in the URL of the current document.

Although the implementation of a full-featured proxy is technically feasible to view existing annotations, a severe drawback happens when it comes to creating new annotations. The proxy has virtually no control over the loaded pages. When the user needs to attach an annotation to a specific text in the document, the system first needs to identify this point in the document. The text itself is not sufficient for that : it may appear many times in the document. Several methods have been tried. Some systems prompt the user to manually paste the text in a dialog box, checking it appears only once in the complete document (Yee, 1998). In our experiments, we found that this is a real burden for users. Other systems require that the users load the page being annotated in a separate HTML editor where the user inserts the annotation. By calculating the difference between the new version and the original document content, the system is thus able to get the proper annotation anchor and attributes. Again, creating an annotation is a very challenging process for the user.

The last module is the storage of the annotations. Since annotations may be shared, a typical approach is to store them on a remotely accessible server. Most systems generally provide three kinds of annotations : public, group and private annotations. Even private annotations are kept on the annotation server. Firstly, the design of the annotation system is basically the same, and secondly the annotation attributes can be easily changed so that become public for instance. But this approach rises again the issue of privacy. Moreover, contacting the annotation server adds a significant delay when browsing the Internet. Our evaluation of existing annotation systems showed that users do not feel comfortable to wait when they want to create personal annotations. However, they are willing to accept such delays when creating group or public annotations.

How the Document Object Model Level 2 Improves Web Annotation Systems

Despite the disadvantages of a proxy-based intermediary, many annotation systems relied on this technology because it was browser independent. But new technologies - the Document Object Model Level 2 and Dynamic HTML (W3C, 1999a) - are now being used and will change drastically the design of Web annotation systems. Since this technology is implemented in a very popular commercial Web browser – namely Internet Explorer - , it has already been used in several recent commercial products like ThirdVoice, iMarkup, Expression-net and uTOK.

With the Document Object Model (DOM), an application can easily manipulate the content of a document. Compared with its old version, the DOM level 2 adds the range objects. A range is a subpart of a document, for instance the text which is selected by the user. The advantage for an annotation system is immediate : through the range object and the DOM, the system can precisely locate the annotation anchor in the document. The range object is very important when the user has selected a text which appears several times in the document. In this case, the annotation system needs to precisely locate the position of the selection and compute which occurrence has been selected. Otherwise, it would be unable to insert the annotation properly. Once the right occurrence has been found, the annotation system can dynamically change its layout without forcing the browser to reload the entire document. For instance, the system may simply change the color of the selected text.

Compared to existing systems, the advantages of the DOM level 2 are quite clear for users : creating an annotation is as easy as selecting the text in the document and click on a special option in the browser.. Our experiment with Yawas also showed that XML files can be processed the same way. But to manipulate the DOM, the annotation system first needs to get its interface. Historically, the DOM was only accessible to scripting languages like JavaScript. Moreover, these scripts had to be embedded in the documents to be able to modify them. Of course, this is not of much help for an annotation system unless it uses some tricks to automatically embed the scripts in every page. Again, one approach is to use a proxy-like intermediary which inserts the scripts in every page before they are sent to the browser. This has been used in CritLink (Yee, 1998) and InterNote (Vasudevan, 1999). But a better approach would be for the browser to provide an API making the DOM accessible to external applications.

The last version of Internet Explorer provides such an API. An external program written as an ActiveX object can use this interface to access and modify the documents loaded in the browser. The object first registers to Internet Explorer. Each new instance of Internet Explorer will then launch an instance of this ActiveX object, giving it the DOM interface of any document which will be subsequently loaded. Moreover, Internet Explorer provides event notification interfaces : the ActiveX objects can thus be notified of any event occurring in the browser. Among these events, the *beforenavigate2* and *documentcomplete* events are important for the annotation system. The first one notifies the annotation system of the document being requested by the user. Instead of waiting for the document to be retrieved from the Internet, the annotation system can start to retrieve the annotations attached to this document since it knows its URL. When it receives the *documentcomplete* event, the annotation system then modifies the layout of the document to insert the annotations. Work is under way at W3C to make the DOM accessible to external applications and we can expect that major Web browsers will support this functionality.

Another way to get the DOM is to extend the context menu of Internet Explorer. To each option is associated a script which has access to the DOM. Our annotation system uses this method since it is much easier. We detail it in the next section. To our knowledge, two recent systems already use this facility, ThirdVoice and iMarkup. The first one may be considered as a public annotation system, although personal notes may be stored on the server. On the other hand, iMarkup is designed for the personal use. It remains possible to share annotated documents by email with other users having the software installed on their machine. The interface shows the powerful capabilities of DOM level 2: users can create inline annotations, post-it notes and draw free-form shapes on the screen.

Remaining Challenges for Annotations Systems

The annotation systems powered by the DOM Level 2 and Dynamic HTML are much better than the previous proxy-based systems. But all the challenges have not been addressed so far. It is out of the scope of this chapter to discuss them in detail, but the issues are important. The first one is privacy (Marshall, 1998). With an annotation tool, users don't only show their navigational habits, but also select the words they like or dislike. Of course, a centralized server may be hazardous especially if a privately held company owns the annotation database. We will show hereafter how annotations can improve information access through personalized document clustering ; other research (Golovchinsky, 1998) already proved how they can improve information retrieval. For privacy concerns, we chose to build our annotation system with a 100% client approach. Users can still share their annotations by email and even publish them on a Web server. Like with bookmarks, this design seems obvious when the annotation system is preliminary used to create personal annotations. It may be different when the system is used to share annotations between a group of coworkers. However, we suggest that the process of annotating is very similar to the one used when creating bookmarks. In a first step, users create personal bookmarks. They may then select some of them and share this list by creating a Web page.

Another issue that annotation systems should address in the future is interoperability. Today, every single annotation system uses a different way to represent the annotations, beginning with the annotation anchors. XPointers (W3C, 1999c) have been proposed for XML documents, CritLink stores the selected text, and Yawas adds the occurrence of the selected text. A detailed discussion appears in (Phelps, 2000a) where the authors propose new ways to represent the annotation anchor. Their proposition not only applies to XML documents, but also to HTML, PostScript and PDF documents.

In the following section, we present our Web annotation system, called Yawas for Yet Another Web Annotation System.

PRESENTATION OF YAWAS

Yawas is a prototype annotation system written in Java and JavaScript. It was designed to study how the annotations can be used to improve current bookmarks. After having reviewed the existing annotation systems, Yawas has been designed with the following properties :

- Users can highlight and annotate specific texts in a document, not only the whole document
- Annotations are stored locally for privacy and speed concerns
- Unlike most existing systems, highlighting a text is fast and easy
- Yawas works with a popular Web browser (currently Internet Explorer) so that users don't have to change their habits
- Unlike other proxy-based systems, local and remote documents can be annotated

Hereafter, we present the architecture of the system and a typical usage scenario.

ARCHITECTURE OF THE SYSTEM

The system is made of two separate layers. The first one includes the scripts which have access to the Document Object Model. Since they have access to the DOM, they are used to process the documents. This layer is highly platform and browser dependent. The second layer is used for annotation storage, retrieval and the search engine. It is implemented in Java and is thus browser and platform independent. The two layers communicate by using the HTTP protocol.

The different options of Yawas are called with a simple mouse click in the context menu of the browser. The context menu of Internet Explorer can be easily extended by adding an entry in the registry file. For the prototype, it was preferred to more complicated ActiveX objects. To each option of this context menu is then associated a script written in JavaScript. Using a special ActiveX object provided with the Windows operating system, each script can use the HTTP protocol to exchange data with the second layer. The scripts are typically used to retrieve the document URL and title, parent URL, selection and occurrence number. They are also used to modify the layout of the document by highlighting the annotation anchors in yellow. The DOM is retrieved from the external arguments provided to the scripts by Internet Explorer (figure 1). Since the scripts know the current selection through a *range object,* they can change its color. A typical example is shown in figure 2.

```
<script language="javascript">
var parentwin = external.menuArguments;
var doc = parentwin.document;
var url = external.menuArguments.location.href;
var selection_range = doc.selection.createRange();
var selected_text = selection_range.text;
var document_range = doc.body.createTextRange();
var fulltext = document_range.text;
...
...any further processing here...
</script>
```

Fig 1: Getting the Document url, Selection and Document Body from the External Arguments

```
<script language="javascript">
var parentwin = external.menuArguments;
var doc = external.menuArguments.document;
...
document.selection.createRange().execCommand("BackColor",0,"yellow");
...
</script>
```

Figure 2: using the DOM and Dynamic HTML

There could be more than one annotation attached to a specific text in a document. When a "Delete" command is received, the Java application returns an HTML document with the list of the annotations attached to this specified text. The user can choose the one to delete and this choice is sent through HTTP to the Java application.

Similarly, "View" returns the list of the annotations attached to a specific document. The script searches each annotation anchor in the current document and highlight them in yellow. The other attributes of the annotations are displayed in a separate window.

The "Query" command is different from "View" in the sense that it returns an HTML document readily formatted to be displayed in a Web browser. Examples are shown in figure 7. Since the communication with the Java application is established using the HTTP protocol, the application could be located anywhere on the internet. By default, it is running on the local machine for privacy and efficiency reasons. But if installed on a remotely accessible machine, the Java application can be used to share the same annotation set. Users are still required to install the scripts and extend their context menu.

We now detail a typical usage scenario where users create, retrieve and share their annotation using Yawas.

RETRIEVING ANNOTATIONS AND DOCUMENTS

Yawas also offers a search engine to retrieve the annotations. The search engine is part of the second layer implemented in Java and is thus platform and browser independent. It can be seen as a light Web server and can be accessed from the local machine through a standard Web browser. This Java application listen to a specific port on the local machine. For efficiency reasons, the search engine loads the complete annotation set in memory.

In the current interface, Yawas displays a form with all the annotation attributes (figure 8). Some attributes are taken from a controlled list which is stored in the configuration file:

- Document topics (e.g. classification, clustering, finance, ...)
- Document types (e.g. scientific paper, newspaper, personal home page, ...)
- Selection types (e.g. person's name, software, date, definition, ...)
- Annotation styles (e.g. agree, disagree, *, **, ***, ...)

This list is easily customizable to meet users' needs. Each attribute values are arranged in a list box so that users can easily build their queries. The "selection" and "comment" attribute respectively let users search in the highlighted texts and in the comments of each annotation. The "document type" attribute has been created in order to separate document types and topics. A rapid survey of bookmark files showed that many users tend to create categories which are types of documents. Since a document has both a type (e.g. scientific paper) and a topic (e.g. document classification), these users should in theory duplicate the same bookmark in the two categories. But this is rarely applied in practice and the bookmarks become inconsistent. In the current version, the result of the search engine is a list of the annotations clustered by document URL.

SHARING ANNOTATIONS

To share annotations, the user selects the options "Import" or "Export" available in the context menu. When "Export" is chosen, Yawas retrieves all the annotations attached to the current document and builds a string made by the document URL and the concatenation of the annotation anchors. We call this string an *extended URL*. Since annotation anchors can be very long, Yawas only keeps 1) the 10 first and 10 last characters, 2) the length of the annotation anchor, and 3) its occurrence in the complete document. For instance, the first phrase of this paragraph "To share annotations, ... context menu" is encoded as follow :To+share+a&ntext+menu&101&0, where 101 is the length of the string and 0 the occurrence of this string in the complete document. If this document was published on http://localhost/papers/riao2000.html, the resulting *extended URL* generated by yawas would look like : http://localhost/papers/riao2000.html#To+share+a&ntext menu&101&0.

If more than one annotation is attached to a document, their corresponding strings are concatenated. How to encode an annotation anchor is a research topic and we may change our current implementation in the future. However, once this string has been displayed, the user can copy and paste it anywhere, like an email or a Web document. It is the same as copying a URL, although the extended URLs are not useable in current Web browsers. To import such extended URLs, the users thus need to choose the option "Import" and paste the extended URL where Yawas prompts it. Yawas loads the document in the current browser Window and modifies its content so that annotation anchors are highlighted in green. Another option to share the annotations among a group of users is to configure the server application so that it can be reached over the network. In its current implementation, Yawas does not check users' names and a robust Web server should be preferred in this case.

CURRENT LIMITATIONS

Because Yawas extends the contextual menu, every script is run upon user's request. As a result, existing annotations do not appear automatically and the user needs to explicitly select the "View" option in the context menu to see them. Although this was not perceived as a severe limitation by most users, we plan to modify the current implementation in a near future. Yawas will use ActiveX objects which extend Internet Explorer and are able to sink all the events as explained before.

Experiments and Results

Yawas is extensively used by the authors, our team of 7 researchers and 18 masters' students in computer science. The authors and our team are using Yawas instead of the bookmark tools provided with their browser. The students used it during their work where they annotated about 50 documents. We now report on several experiments in which we evaluated the user's interface and the use of annotations to improve information access and retrieval.

User's Interface Evalutation

The most appreciated points are the fast and dynamic creation of annotations and the respect of privacy. Most users appreciated the similarity between highlighting a printed document and highlighting a Web document with Yawas. Most users did not take time to fill in the form opened when creating a new annotation. They extensively used the "highlight" option which just highlights the selected text without prompting other information. Like bookmarks, this suggests that automatic clustering or classification could be needed to organize the documents.

With Yawas, users first reduce the cognitive overload when they retrieve a document previously annotated, which is an improvement over bookmarks. Users reported that navigating from the annotations to the document was useful : they didn't have to manually browse the document to see the highlighted texts. Moreover, the window displaying the annotation anchors was useful to get a personalized view of the document.

Using Annotations to Improve Document Clustering

We asked a human classifier to manually cluster a set of 350 documents highlighted by someone else. The classifier was asked to cluster the documents using either the original document, or only the highlighted texts. From 350 documents, 32 document URLs were no longer valid. Since the documents could not be retrieved, the classifier was obviously unable to classify these pages, but was still able to classify them when using the highlighted texts.

When clustering the documents, the classifier chose to create cluster names. Interestingly, the number of clusters was statistically the same in both experiments (about 37), but the names created when considering only the highlighted texts were a lot more precise. Typical examples include "conference" instead of the more precise "classification", and "home page" instead of "annotation". The clustering produced by the human classifier was compared to the clustering made by the creator of the annotations. The classifier did 35 mistakes when using the full text of the documents, and only 5 mistakes when using the highlighted texts. It is not surprising since many documents are index pages where a few lines are of interest to a particular user. Typical examples which appear in the annotations we collected include Web pages with scientific publications, software listings, music files and news. Using the annotation tool, a user can highlight these meaningful words.

This experiment suggests that the highlighted texts can improve the automatic clustering of Web pages, and thus help users to classify their bookmarks in a personalized way. More importantly, it shows that storing the full text is not necessary when performing clustering on annotated documents :

highlighted texts may be enough. This is important since it drastically reduces the time to cluster the documents.

Using Annotations to Improve Information Access and Retrieval

An evaluation with 18 masters' students has been undertaken. The students were divided in two equal groups. Each group had to write a report on a given subject, which required the reading of at least 20 documents. During the experiment, 50 documents were actually read and highlighted. The students could not speak to each other directly: they only had the right to use bookmarks, email and a shared word processor using NetMeeting. Only one group could use Yawas. They shared the same annotation server, thus allowing a cooperative annotation of the documents.

After three months, when the students had to write their report, annotations have been extensively used as a way to summarize the documents. After the document title and document type, the search engine provided with Yawas returns the concatenation of the texts highlighted in each document. When the query is empty, the search engine returns the complete set of documents. This functionality was used to get the summaries of all the documents.

Several students did not need to access the full text of the document to retrieve what they were looking for. This result suggests that the highlighted texts can improve information access and retrieval. The group who used a traditional bookmark was obviously unable to produce such summaries. Although not allowed in the experiment, students in this group printed the documents and annotated them. The students also extensively used Yawas to score the documents. Yawas was customized so that ratings (*, **, ***) could be attached to each annotation. Yawas has also been extensively used to know what other students had already read. This result confirms that annotations have a clear value to future readers (Marshall, 1998).

FUTURE WORK

Automatic document clustering has already been applied

on the document set consisting of 350 documents and 1200 annotation anchors. Hierarchical agglomerative clustering was used as in (Mareek, 1996). Although more comparisons are required, our preliminary results show that annotation-based clustering is better at identifying similar documents compared to a full text clustering. However, many small clusters were found in the annotation-based clustering and a mixture of both methods is now under way. For instance, greater importance could be given to the highlighted words. A similar approach has successfully been applied in (Weiss, 1996) where greater weights were given to the words contained inside specific HTML tags like <TITLE>, <H1>, <H2> and <address>. After an initial clustering has been proposed to the users, newly highlighted documents should be properly inserted into this existing classification. We are studying how the annotations can help. A problem occurs when a document is highlighted for the first time : the automatic classifier is given little information. We suggest to boost the classifier with the words already highlighted in the classified documents. We thus give the classifier more information to compute a similarity with the other documents. When there is no existing classification scheme, (Li, 1998) suggested to use Internet search engines as automatic classifiers. The advantage of using an existing search engine is to get a meaningful category name since they are manually selected. To classify a document, the method selects significant words from the document and then issues a query to the search engine. Significant words are usually selected using word frequency and inverse document frequency. The search engine then returns the documents found similar to this request along with their category. Similarly, we will use the highlighted texts as significant words and see how the classification changes. We expect it to be more user-directed. Even if existing search engines could be used to find the topic of a document, this approach should be combined with a more traditional approach where user defined categories are considered. With Yawas, each annotation has an attribute called "document type". Examples include "scientific paper", "home page", "discussion forum", "news"... These user defined categories do not necessary exist in existing search engines.

Preliminary results also showed that annotations can be used to summarize the documents. Recent research in automatic document summarization (Lopez, 1999 ; Tombros, 1998) demonstrated the benefits of using query terms to produce personalized document summaries. Similarly, highlighted texts could be used to build user-directed document summaries. Document summaries are important for information access and the simple concatenation of highlighted texts has proved to be useful in one of our experiments. When using a search engine, these annotation-based summaries are used to decide if a document should be read or not. In a future experiment, we will measure users' speed and accuracy in classifying documents when they use the annotation-based summaries or more typical summaries like the title and first few sentences of the documents.

CONCLUSION

We implemented and tested Yawas, a new Web annotation system. Speed and privacy are important issues when personal annotations are involved. The DOM Level 2 is necessary to access and process the annotated documents in an efficient way. Unlike most systems, the annotations are stored locally for speed and privacy reasons.

The annotation system offers many advantages over the current bookmark programs used in Web browsers. First, the annotations reduce the information overload since users can personalize the documents they read. Second, users can easily share their annotations by email. Third, highlighted texts can be used to present user-directed document summaries.

8

Internet Protocols

INTRODUCTION

The Internet protocols are the world's most popular open-system (non-proprietary) protocol suite because they can be used to communicate across any set of interconnected networks and are equally well suited for LAN and WAN communications. The Internet protocols consist of a suite of communication protocols, of which the two best known are the Transmission Control Protocol (TCP) and the Internet Protocol (IP). The Internet protocol suite not only includes lower-layer protocols (such as TCP and IP), but it also specifies common applications such as electronic mail, terminal emulation, and file transfer.

This chapter provides a broad introduction to specifications that comprise the Internet protocols. Discussions include IP addressing and key upper-layer protocols used in the Internet. Specific routing protocols are addressed individually in Part 6, Routing Protocols. Internet protocols were first developed in the mid-1970s, when the Defence Advanced Research Projects Agency (DARPA) became interested in establishing a packet-switched network that would facilitate communication between dissimilar computer systems at research institutions.

With the goal of heterogeneous connectivity in mind, DARPA funded research by Stanford University and Bolt, Beranek, and Newman (BBN). The result of this development effort was the Internet protocol suite, completed in the late

1970s. TCP/IP later was included with Berkeley Software Distribution (BSD) UNIX and has since become the foundation on which the Internet and the World Wide Web (WWW) are based. Documentation of the Internet protocols (including new or revised protocols) and policies are specified in technical reports called Request For Comments (RFCs), which are published and then reviewed and analysed by the Internet community. Protocol refinements are published in the new RFCs. To illustrate the scope of the Internet protocols, figure maps many of the protocols of the Internet protocol suite and their corresponding OSI layers. This chapter addresses the basic elements and operations of these and other key Internet protocols.

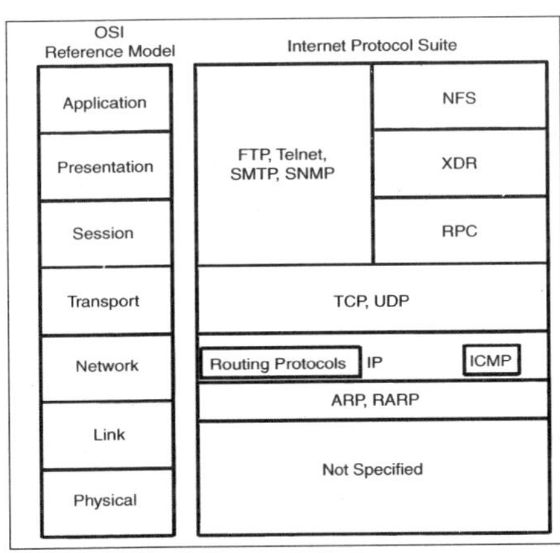

Fig 8.1 Internet Protocols Span the Complete Range of OSI Model Layers

The Internet Protocol (IP) is a network-layer (Layer 3) protocol that contains addressing information and some control information that enables packets to be routed. IP is documented in RFC 791 and is the primary network-layer protocol in the Internet protocol suite. Along with the Transmission Control Protocol (TCP), IP represents the heart of the Internet protocols. IP has two primary responsibilities: providing connectionless, best-effort delivery of datagrams through an internetwork; and providing fragmentation and reassembly of datagrams to support data links with different maximum-transmission unit (MTU) sizes.

IP PACKET FORMAT

An IP packet contains several types of information, as illustrated in figure.

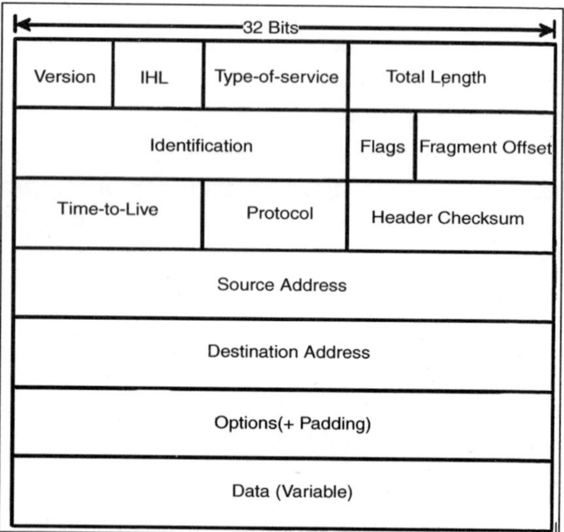

Fig 8.2 Fourteen Fields Comprise and IP Packet

The following discussion describes the IP packet fields:

- *Version*—Indicates the version of IP currently used.
- *IP Header Length* (IHL)—Indicates the datagram header length in 32-bit words.
- *Type-of-Service*—Specifies how an upper-layer protocol would like a current datagram to be handled, and assigns datagrams various levels of importance.
- *Total Length*—Specifies the length, in bytes, of the entire IP packet, including the data and header.
- *Identification*—Contains an integer that identifies the current datagram. This field is used to help piece together datagram fragments.
- *Flags*—Consists of a 3-bit field of which the two low-order (least-significant) bits control fragmentation. The low-order bit specifies whether the packet can be fragmented. The middle bit specifies whether the

packet is the last fragment in a series of fragmented packets. The third or high-order bit is not used.

- *Fragment Offset*—Indicates the position of the fragment's data relative to the beginning of the data in the original datagram, which allows the destination IP process to properly reconstruct the original datagram.
- *Time-to-Live*—Maintains a counter that gradually decrements down to zero, at which point the datagram is discarded. This keeps packets from looping endlessly.
- *Protocol*—Indicates which upper-layer protocol receives incoming packets after IP processing is complete.
- *Header Checksum*—Helps ensure IP header integrity.
- *Source Address*—Specifies the sending node.
- *Destination Address*—Specifies the receiving node.
- *Options*—Allows IP to support various options, such as security.
- *Data*—Contains upper-layer information.

IP ADDRESSING

As with any other network-layer protocol, the IP addressing scheme is integral to the process of routing IP datagrams through an internetwork. Each IP address has specific components and follows a basic format. These IP addresses can be subdivided and used to create addresses for sub networks.

Each host on a TCP/IP network is assigned a unique 32-bit logical address that is divided into two main parts: the network number and the host number. The network number identifies a network and must be assigned by the Internet Network Information Center (InterNIC) if the network is to be part of the Internet. An Internet Service Provider (ISP) can obtain blocks of network addresses from the InterNIC and can itself assign address space as necessary. The host number identifies a host on a network and is assigned by the local network administrator.

IP Address Format

The 32-bit IP address is grouped eight bits at a time, separated by dots, and represented in decimal format (known as *dotted decimal notation*). Each bit in the octet has a binary weight (128, 64, 32, 16, 8, 4, 2, 1). The minimum value for an octet is 0, and the maximum value for an octet is 255.

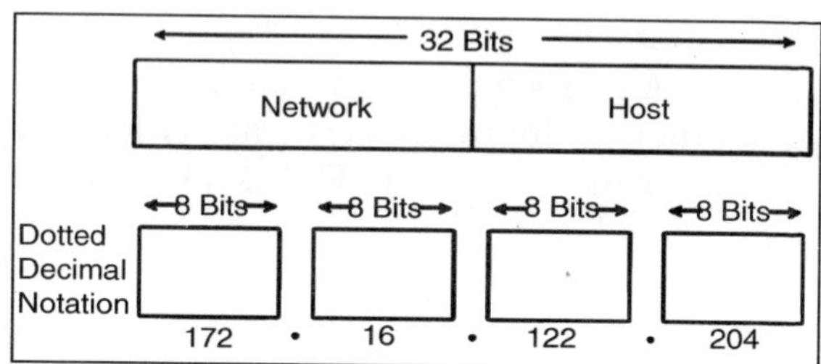

Fig 8.3 Illustrates the Basic Format of Asn IP Address

IP ADDRESS CLASSES

IP addressing supports five different address classes: A, B,C, D, and E. Only classes A, B, and C are available for commercial use. The left-most (high-order) bits indicate the network class. Table provides reference information about the five IP address classes.

Table 8.1 Reference Information about the Five IP Address Classes

IP Address Class	Format	Purpose	High-order Bit(s)	Address Range	No. Bits Network/Host	Max. Hosts
A	N.H.H.H[1]	Few large Organization	0	1.0.0.0 to 126.0.0.0.	7/24	16,777, 214[2] (2^{24}–2)
B	N.N.H.H	Medium-size Organization	1,0	128.1.0.0 to 191.254.0.0	14/16	65,543 (2^{16}–2)
C	N.N.N.H	Relatively small organization	1,1,0	192.0.1.0 to 223.255.254.0	22/8	245 (2^{8}–2)
D	N/A	Multicast groups (RFC 1112)	1,1,1,0	224.0.0.0 to 239.255.255.255	N/A (not for commercial use)	N/A
E	N/A	Experimental	1,1,1,1	240.0.0.0 to 254.255.255.255	N/A	N/A

Notes:

1 N = Network number, H = Host number

2 One address is reserved for the braodcast address, and one address is reserved for the network.

Figure illustrates the format of the commercial IP address classes. (Note the high-order bits in each class.)

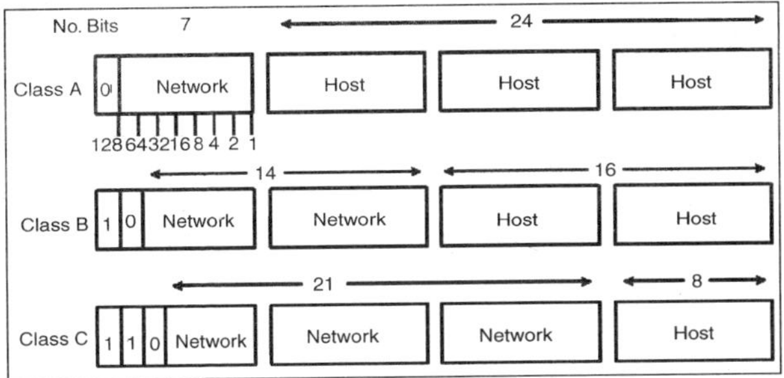

Fig 8.4 IP Address Formats A, B, and C are Available for Commercial Use

Address Class	First Octet in Decimal	High-Order Bits
Class A	1 Ð 126	0
Class B	128 Ð 191	10
Class C	192 Ð 223	110
Class D	224 Ð 239	1110
Class E	240 Ð 254	1111

Fig 8.5 A Range of Possible Values Exists for the First Octet of each Address Class

The class of address can be determined easily by examining the first octet of the address and mapping that value to a class range in the following table. In an IP address of 172.31.1.2, for example, the first octet is 172. Because 172 falls between 128 and 191, 172.31.1.2 is a Class B address.

Figure summarises the range of possible values for the first octet of each address class.

IP Subnet Addressing

IP networks can be divided into smaller networks called subnetworks (or subnets). Subnetting provides the network administrator with several benefits, including extra flexibility, more efficient use of network addresses, and the capability to contain broadcast traffic (a broadcast will not cross a router). Subnets are under local administration. As such, the outside world sees an organisation as a single network and has no detailed knowledge of the organisation's internal structure. A given network address can be broken up into many subnetworks. For example, 172.16.1.0, 172.16.2.0, 172.16.3.0, and 172.16.4.0 are all subnets within network 171.16.0.0. (All 0s in the host portion of an address specifies the entire network.)

IP Subnet Mask

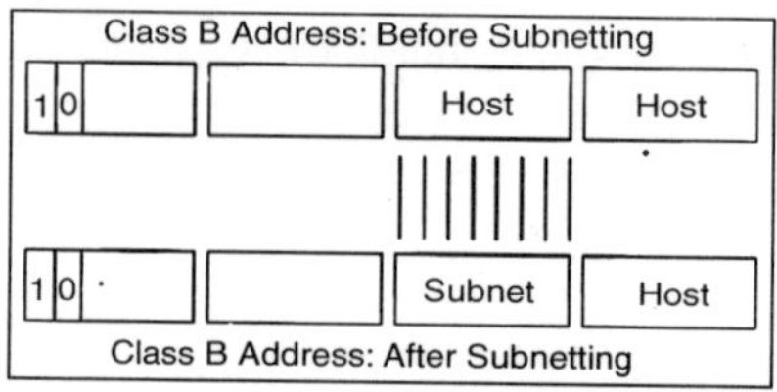

Fig 8.6 Bits are Borrowed from the Host Address Field to Create the Subnet Address Field

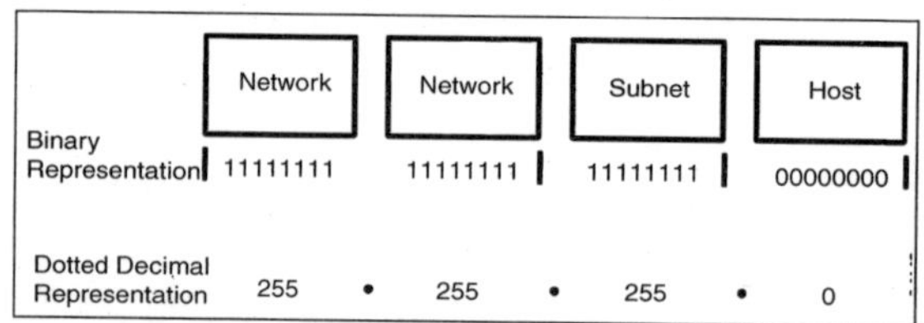

Fig 8.7 A Sample Subnet Mask Consists of all Binary 1s and 0s

A subnet address is created by "borrowing" bits from the host field and designating them as the subnet field. The number of borrowed bits varies and is specified by the subnet mask. Figure shows how bits are borrowed from the host address field to create the subnet address field.

Subnet masks use the same format and representation technique as IP addresses. The subnet mask, however, has binary 1s in all bits specifying the network and subnetwork fields, and binary 0s in all bits specifying the host field. Figure illustrates a sample subnet mask.

Subnet mask bits should come from the high-order (left-most) bits of the host field. Details of Class B and C subnet mask types follow. Class A addresses are not discussed in this chapter because they generally are subnetted on an 8-bit boundary.

128	64	32	16	8	4	2	1		
1	0	0	0	0	0	0	0	=	128
1	1	0	0	0	0	0	0	=	192
1	1	1	0	0	0	0	0	=	224
1	1	1	1	0	0	0	0	=	240
1	1	1	1	1	0	0	0	=	248
1	1	1	1	1	1	0	0	=	252
1	1	1	1	1	1	1	0	=	254
1	1	1	1	1	1	1	1	=	255

Fig 8.8 Subnet Mask Bits come from the High-order Bits of the Host Field

Various types of subnet masks exist for Class B and C subnets. The default subnet mask for a Class B address that has no subnetting is 255.255.0.0, while the subnet mask for a Class B address 171.16.0.0 that specifies eight bits of subnetting is 255.255.255.0. The reason for this is that eight bits of subnetting or $2^8 - 2$ (1 for the network address and 1 for the broadcast address) = 254 subnets possible, with $2^8 - 2 = 254$ hosts per subnet.

Table 8.2 Class B Subnetting Reference Chart

Number of Bits	Subnet Mask	Number of Subnets	Number of Hosts
2	255.255.192.0	2	16382
3	255.255.224.0	6	8190
4	255.255.240.0	14	4094
5	255.255.248.0	30	2046
6	255.255.252.0	62	1022
7	255.255.254.0	126	510
8	255.255.255.0	254	254
9	255.255.255.128	510	126
10	255.255.255.192	1022	62
11	255.255.255.224	2046	30
12	255.255.255.240	4094	14
13	255.255.255.248	8190	6
14	255.255.255.252	16382	2

Table 8.3 Class C Subnetting Reference Chart

Number of Bits	Subnet Mask	Number of Subnets	Number of Hosts
2	255.255.255.192	2	62

3	255.255.255.224	6	30
4	255.255.255.240	14	14
5	255.255.255.248	30	6
6	255.255.255.252	62	2

The subnet mask for a Class C address 192.168.2.0 that specifies five bits of subnetting is 255.255.255.248.With five bits available for subnetting, $2^5 - 2 = 30$ subnets possible, with $2^3 - 2 = 6$ hosts per subnet. The reference charts shown in tables can be used when planning Class B and C networks to determine the required number of subnets and hosts, and the appropriate subnet mask.

How Subnet Masks are Used to Determine the Network Number

The router performs a set process to determine the network (or more specifically, the subnetwork) address. First, the router extracts the IP destination address from the incoming packet and retrieves the internal subnet mask. It then performs a *logical AND* operation to obtain the network number.

This causes the host portion of the IP destination address to be removed, while the destination network number remains. The router then looks up the destination network number and matches it with an outgoing interface. Finally, it forwards the frame to the destination IP address.

Logical and Operation

Three basic rules govern logically "ANDing" two binary numbers. First, 1 "ANDed" with 1 yields 1. Second, 1 "ANDed" with 0 yields 0. Finally, 0 "ANDed" with 0 yields 0. The truth table provided in table illustrates the rules for logical AND operations.

Table 8.4 Rules for Logical and Operations

Input	Input	Output
1	1	1
1	0	0
0	1	0
0	0	0

Two simple guidelines exist for remembering logical AND operations: Logically "ANDing" a 1 with a 1 yields the original value, and logically "ANDing" a 0 with any number yields 0. Figure illustrates that when a logical AND of the destination IP address and the subnet mask is performed, the subnetwork number remains, which the router uses to forward the packet.

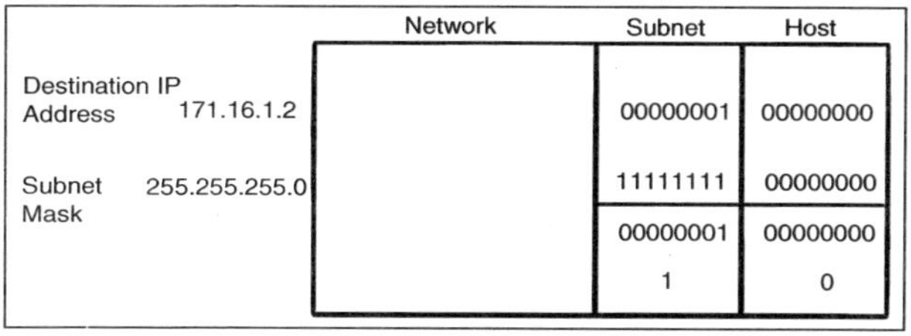

		Network	Subnet	Host
Destination IP Address	171.16.1.2		00000001	00000000
Subnet Mask	255.255.255.0		11111111	00000000
			00000001	00000000
			1	0

Fig 8.9 Applying a Logical and the Destination IP Address and the Subnet Mask Produces the Subnetwork Number

ADDRESS RESOLUTION PROTOCOL (ARP)

For two machines on a given network to communicate, they must know the other machine's physical (orMAC) addresses. By broadcasting Address Resolution Protocols (ARPs), a host can dynamically discover the MAC-layer address corresponding to a particular IP network-layer address.

After receiving aMAC-layer address, IP devices create an ARP cache to store the recently acquired IP-to-MAC address mapping, thus avoiding having to broadcast ARPS when they want to recontact a device. If the device does not respond within a specified time frame, the cache entry is flushed. In addition to the Reverse Address Resolution Protocol (RARP) is used to mapMAC-layer addresses to IP addresses. RARP, which is the logical inverse of ARP, might be used by diskless workstations that do not know their IP addresses when they boot. RARP relies on the presence of a RARP server with table entries of MAC-layer-to-IP address mappings.

INTERNET ROUTING

Internet routing devices traditionally have been called gateways. In today's terminology, however, the term gateway refers specifically to a device that performs application-layer protocol translation between devices. Interior gateways refer to devices that perform these protocol functions between machines or networks under the same administrative control or authority, such as a corporation's internal network. These are known as autonomous systems.

Exterior gateways perform protocol functions between independent networks. Routers within the Internet are organised hierarchically. Routers used for information exchange within autonomous systems are called interior routers, which use a variety of Interior Gateway Protocols (IGPs) to accomplish this purpose. The Routing Information Protocol (RIP) is an example of an IGP. Routers that move information between autonomous systems are called exterior routers. These routers use an exterior gateway protocol to exchange information between autonomous systems. The Border Gateway Protocol (BGP) is an example of an exterior gateway protocol.

IP ROUTING

IP routing protocols are dynamic. Dynamic routing calls for routes to be calculated automatically at regular intervals by software in routing devices. This contrasts with static routing, where routers are established by the network administrator and do not change until the network administrator changes them. An IP routing table, which consists of destination address/next hop pairs, is used to enable dynamic routing. An entry in this table, for example, would be interpreted as follows: to get to network 172.31.0.0, send the packet out Ethernet interface 0 (E0). IP routing specifies that IP datagrams travel through internetworks one hop at a time. The entire route is not known at the onset of the journey, however. Instead, at each stop, the next destination is calculated by matching the destination address within the datagram with an entry in the current node's routing table. Each node's involvement in the routing process is limited to forwarding packets based on internal information. The nodes do not monitor whether the packets get to their final destination, nor does IP provide for error reporting back to the source when routing anomalies occur.

INTERNET CONTROL MESSAGE PROTOCOL (ICMP)

The *Internet Control Message Protocol (ICMP)* is a network-layer Internet protocol that provides message packets to report errors and other information regarding IP packet processing back to the source. ICMP is documented in RFC 792.

ICMP MESSAGES

ICMPs generate several kinds of useful messages, including Destination Unreachable, Echo Request and Reply, Redirect, Time Exceeded, and Router Advertisement and Router Solicitation. If an ICMP message cannot be delivered, no second one is generated. This is to avoid an endless flood of ICMP messages. When an ICMP destination-unreachable message is sent by a router, it means that the router is unable to send the package to its final destination. The router then discards the original packet.

Two reasons exist for why a destination might be unreachable. Most commonly, the source host has specified a non-existent address. Less frequently, the router does not have a route to the destination. Destination-unreachable messages include four basic types: network unreachable, host unreachable, protocol unreachable, and port unreachable.

- *Network-unreachable messages* usually mean that a failure has occurred in the routing or addressing of a packet.
- *Host-unreachable messages* usually indicates delivery failure, such as a wrong subnet mask.
- *Protocol-unreachable messages* generally mean that the destination does not support the upper-layer protocol specified in the packet.
- *Port-unreachable messages* imply that the TCP socket or port is not available.

An ICMP echo-request message, which is generated by the ping command, is sent by any host to test node reachability across an internetwork.

The ICMP echo-reply message indicates that the node can be successfully reached. An ICMP Redirect message is sent by the router to the source host to stimulate more efficient routing. The router still forwards the original packet to the destination. ICMP redirects allow host routing tables to remain small because it is necessary to know the address of only one router, even if that router does not provide the best path.

Even after receiving an ICMP Redirect message, some devices might continue using the less-efficient route. An ICMP Time-exceeded message is sent by the router if an IP packet's Time-to-Live field (expressed in hops or seconds) reaches zero. The Time-to-Live field prevents packets from continuously circulating the internetwork if the internetwork contains a routing loop. The router then discards the original packet.

ICMP ROUTER-DISCOVERY PROTOCOL (IDRP)

IDRP uses Router-Advertisement and Router-Solicitation messages to discover the addresses of routers on directly attached subnets. Each router periodically multicasts Router-Advertisement messages from each of its interfaces. Hosts then discover addresses of routers on directly attached subnets by listening for these messages. Hosts can use Router-Solicitation messages to request immediate advertisements rather than waiting for unsolicited messages.

IRDP offers several advantages over other methods of discovering addresses of neighbouring routers. Primarily, it does not require hosts to recognise routing protocols, nor does it require manual configuration by an administrator. Router-Advertisement messages enable hosts to discover the existence of neighbouring routers, but not which router is best to reach a particular destination. If a host uses a poor first-hop router to reach a particular destination, it receives a Redirect message identifying a better choice.

TRANSMISSION CONTROL PROTOCOL (TCP)

The TCP provides reliable transmission of data in an IP environment. TCP corresponds to the transport layer (Layer 4) of the OSI reference model. Among the services TCP provides are stream data transfer, reliability, efficient flow control, full-duplex operation, and multiplexing. With stream data transfer, TCP delivers an unstructured stream of bytes identified by sequence numbers. This service benefits applications because they do not have to chop data into blocks before handing it off to TCP.

Instead, TCP groups bytes into segments and passes them to IP for delivery. TCP offers reliability by providing connection-oriented, end-to-end reliable packet delivery through an internetwork. It does this by sequencing bytes with a forwarding acknowledgment number that indicates to the destination the next byte the source expects to receive. Bytes not acknowledged within a specified time period are retransmitted.

The reliability mechanism of TCP allows devices to deal with lost, delayed, duplicate, or misread packets. A time-out mechanism allows devices to detect lost packets and request retransmission. TCP offers efficient flow control, which means that, when sending acknowledgments back to the source, the receiving TCP process indicates the highest sequence number it can receive without overflowing its internal buffers. Full-duplex operation means that TCP processes can both send and receive at the same time. Finally, TCP's multiplexing means that numerous simultaneous upper-layer conversations can be multiplexed over a single connection.

TCP CONNECTION ESTABLISHMENT

To use reliable transport services, TCP hosts must establish a connection-oriented session with one another. Connection establishment is performed by using a "three-way handshake" mechanism. A three-way handshake synchronises both ends of a connection by allowing both sides to agree upon initial sequence numbers. This mechanism also guarantees that both sides are ready to transmit data and know that the other side is ready to transmit as well. This is necessary so that packets are not transmitted or retransmitted during session establishment or after session termination. Each host randomly chooses a sequence number used to track bytes within the stream it is sending and receiving.

Then, the three-way handshake proceeds in the following manner:

- The first host (Host A) initiates a connection by sending a packet with the initial sequence number (X) and SYN bit set to indicate a connection request.

The second host (Host B) receives the SYN, records the sequence number X, and replies by acknowledging the SYN (with an ACK = X + 1). Host B includes its own initial sequence number (SEQ = Y). An ACK = 20 means the host has received bytes 0 through 19 and expects byte 20 next. This technique is called *forward acknowledgment*. Host A then acknowledges all bytes Host B sent with a forward acknowledgment indicating the next byte Host A expects to receive (ACK = Y + 1). Data transfer then can begin.

POSITIVE ACKNOWLEDGMENT AND RETRANSMISSION (PAR)

A simple transport protocol might implement a reliability-and-flow-control technique where the source sends one packet, starts a timer, and waits for an acknowledgment before sending a new packet. If the acknowledgment is not received before the timer expires, the source retransmits the packet. Such a technique is called *positive acknowledgment and retransmission* (PAR). By assigning each packet a sequence number, PAR enables hosts to track lost or duplicate packets caused by network delays that result in premature retransmission.

The sequence numbers are sent back in the acknowledgments so that the acknowledgments can be tracked. PAR is an inefficient use of bandwidth, however, because a host must wait for an acknowledgment before sending a new packet, and only one packet can be sent at a time.

TCP SLIDING WINDOW

A *TCP sliding window* provides more efficient use of network bandwidth than PAR because it enables hosts to send multiple bytes or packets before waiting for an acknowledgment. In TCP, the receiver specifies the current window size in every packet. Because TCP provides a byte-stream connection, window sizes are expressed in bytes. This means that a window is the number of data bytes that the sender is allowed to send before waiting for an acknowledgment.

Initial window sizes are indicated at connection setup, but might vary throughout the data transfer to provide flow control. A window size of zero, for instance, means "Send no data." In a TCP sliding-window operation, for example, the sender might have a sequence of bytes to send (numbered 1 to 10) to a receiver who has a window size of five. The sender then would place a window around the first five bytes and transmit them together. It would then wait for an acknowledgment.

The receiver would respond with an ACK = 6, indicating that it has received bytes 1 to 5 and is expecting byte 6 next. In the same packet, the receiver would indicate that its window size is 5.

The sender then would move the sliding window five bytes to the right and transmit bytes 6 to 10. The receiver would respond with an ACK = 11, indicating that it is expecting sequenced byte 11 next. In this packet, the receiver might indicate that its window size is 0 (because, for example, its internal buffers are full). At this point, the sender cannot send any more bytes until the receiver sends another packet with a window size greater than 0.

TCP PACKET FORMAT

Figure illustrates the fields and overall format of a TCP packet.

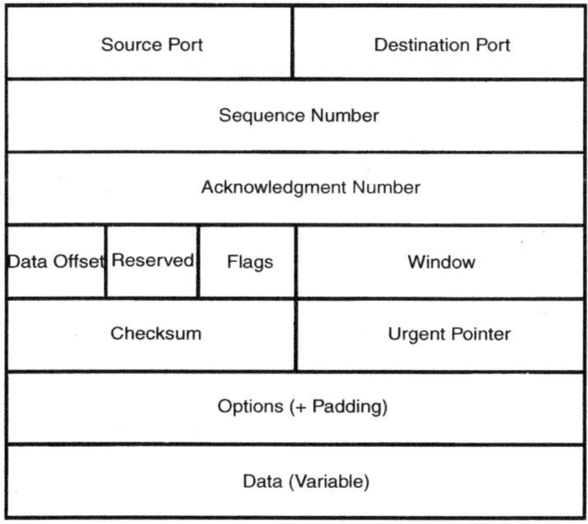

Fig 8.10 Twelve Fields Comprise a TCP Packet

TCP PACKET FIELD DESCRIPTIONS

The following descriptions summarise the TCP packet fields illustrated in figure:

- *Source Port* and *Destination Port*—Identifies points at which upper-layer source and destination processes receive TCP services.
- *Sequence Number*—Usually specifies the number assigned to the first byte of data in the current message. In the connection-establishment phase, this field also can be used to identify an initial sequence number to be used in an upcoming transmission.
- *Acknowledgment Number*—Contains the sequence number of the next byte of data the sender of the packet expects to receive.
- *Data Offset*—Indicates the number of 32-bit words in the TCP header.
- *Reserved*—Remains reserved for future use.
- *Flags*—Carries a variety of control information, including the SYN and ACK bits used for connection establishment, and the FIN bit used for connection termination.
- *Window*—Specifies the size of the sender's receive window (that is, the buffer space available for incoming data).
- *Checksum*—Indicates whether the header was damaged in transit.
- *Urgent Pointer*—Points to the first urgent data byte in the packet.
- *Options*—Specifies various TCP options.
- *Data*—Contains upper-layer information.

USER DATAGRAM PROTOCOL (UDP)

The User Datagram Protocol (UDP) is a connectionless transport-layer protocol (Layer 4) that belongs to the Internet protocol family. UDP is basically an interface between IP and upper-layer processes. UDP protocol ports distinguish multiple applications running on a single device from one another. Unlike the TCP, UDP adds no reliability, flow-control, or error-recovery functions to IP. Because of UDP's simplicity, UDP headers contain fewer bytes and consume less network overhead than TCP. UDP is useful in situations where the reliability mechanisms of TCP are not necessary, such as in cases where a higher-layer protocol might provide error and flow control. UDP is the transport protocol for several well-known application-layer protocols, including Network File System (NFS), Simple Network Management Protocol (SNMP), Domain Name System (DNS), and Trivial File Transfer Protocol (TFTP). The UDP packet format contains four fields, as shown in Figure. These include source and destination ports, length, and checksum fields.

← 32 Bits →	
Source Port	Destination Port
Length	Checksum

Fig 8.11 A UDP Packet Consists of Four Fields

Source and destination ports contain the 16-bit UDP protocol port numbers used to demultiplex datagrams for receiving application-layer processes. A length field specifies the length of the UDP header and data. Checksum provides an (optional) integrity check on the UDP header and data.

INTERNET PROTOCOLS APPLICATION-LAYER PROTOCOLS

The Internet protocol suite includes many application-layer protocols that represent a wide variety of applications, including the following:

- *File Transfer Protocol (FTP:* Moves files between devices
- *Simple Network-Management Protocol (SNMP):* Primarily reports anomalous network conditions and sets network threshold values
- *Telnet:* Serves as a terminal emulation protocol
- *X Windows:* Serves as a distributed windowing and graphics system used for communication between

X terminals and UNIX workstations

- *Network File System (NFS), External Data Representation (XDR), and Remote Procedure Call (RPC):* Work together to enable transparent access to remote network resources
- *Simple Mail Transfer Protocol (SMTP):* Provides electronic mail services
- *Domain Name System (DNS):* Translates the names of network nodes into network addresses.

Table lists these higher-layer protocols and the applications that they support.

Table 8.5 Higher-Layer Protocols and their Applications

Application	Protocols
File transfer	FTP
Terminal emulation	Telnet
Electronic mail	SMTP
Network management	SNMP
Distributed file services	NFS, XDR, RPC, X Windows

9

Bibliographic Displays

INTRODUCTION

Since the introduction of the first Online Public Access Catalogues (OPACs) in the early 1980s, OPACs have revolutionised the operation of public, academic, and special libraries throughout the world and have generated a large body of related research. An OPAC is an automated, searchable bibliographic database which provides access to a library's collection. The bibliographic displays in an OPAC show information about items belonging to the library's collection.

Such items may include monographs, videocassettes, serials, sound recordings, etc. While the bibliographic information is entered into the database according to the standards established by the second edition of the *Anglo-American Cataloguing Rules* (*AACR2*), no such standard exists for the content or appearance of the bibliographic display. However, after fifteen years of OPAC development, interest in standardisation has been heightened as more and more people are exposed to the vast array of diverse OPAC systems in libraries, many of which are accessible on international computer networks, such as the Internet. The creation of a successful bibliographic display should include user participation in the design process.

Research is required to determine the most useful elements for a standard bibliographic display, and how they should appear on the screen. The choice of a particular bibliographic display format should take into consideration the opinions and needs of users, not just user performance. The characteristic which most clearly distinguishes most OPAC bibliographic displays from the format used on 3X5-inch cards in non-computerised catalogues is the use of labels. The words or phrases to the left of the colons (:) are labels. Labels identify the fields of a bibliographic record, such as Title and Author. In the sample bibliographic display, all the labels are in uppercase and leftjustified.

The words on the right side of the colons are the text or the values of the fields. The text in this display is in upper- and lowercase and is placed a few spaces away from the labels. The labels and the text are the main ingredients of a bibliographic display. OPAC designers and librarians must decide which bibliographic information should be provided in a bibliographic display. Only eight bibliographic elements or fields are listed: Author, Title, Edition, Publisher, Physical Description, Other Authors, Subjects, and Cataloguing Source Number.

After deciding on the elements to be displayed, designers have to think about the display format. Display format includes justification, typography, spacing, font, colour, and video effects, such as reverse video. Although omitted in this sample bibliographic display, instructions are usually included in the display to assist users in navigating in the system. The instructions were not shown in the sample display because they were not of interest in the present project. Methods of collecting comments and opinions of users in research are numerous. The most frequently used techniques are questionnaires, interviews, and focus groups. The choice of technique is determined by the objectives and the scope of the study.

Questionnaires are suitable for collecting representative information from a large number of people, while interviews provide detailed, in-depth opinions of a small number of people. Focus groups usually involve more participants than interviews and fewer participants than questionnaires. Unlike interviews, participants in focus groups may help each other elicit and express their opinions as they discuss a topic together. In the field of library and information science, focus groups are generally used to study user satisfaction with library service.

The present study used focus groups to investigate the bibliographic elements that users find more or less useful in bibliographic displays, the bibliographic information that users would like to add to displays, and the bibliographic display format users prefer. One of the goals of the project was to explore the plausibility of using this qualitative research method in designing and assessing computer interfaces in general, as well as to investigate user opinions and suggestions regarding bibliographic displays. This study was the second phase of a larger project.

The main objective of this study was to obtain information on content and screen design. In order to avoid any bias and influence on participants' opinions, the investigators of the larger project decided to select a student with no formal training in library science generally, and cataloguing, specifically, to be the researcher for this study. Thus, a student in the Master of Information Science programme was selected. The researcher also acted as the focus group moderator. Possible similarities and differences between the English and Chinese (Cantonese) speaking OPAC users were of interest in order to take advantage of the researcher's language ability and because of the growing population of the Chinese community in the Greater Toronto Area.

Therefore, library users of these two languages were asked to participate in the focus groups. Morgan (1988) pointed out that communication may be easier for participants of the same age group than for those of large age difference. In this case, different ages might imply differences in experience in using the computer catalogue system. As a result, age was used in grouping participants in the focus groups. Results collected from the focus group study may be used to design a standard bibliographic display which takes the opinions of users of different linguistic backgrounds and of different ages into consideration.

OPAC INTERFACES

The interface of an OPAC links users to the computerised catalogue using menus, commands, search screens, and messages. Designers of OPAC interfaces must take into consideration not only the purpose of the complete system, but of each individual screen. When making design decisions, interface designers should try to facilitate the achievement of the objectives that the library has set for its users and its catalogue. Several researchers have developed guidelines for OPAC interfaces based on general guidelines for computer interfaces such as those provided by Galitz and on the results of user performance studies.

While some researchers advocate increasing the involvement of users in the computer interface development process, few OPACs created in this manner have entered the market. Libraries searching for computerised library catalogues often meet with frustration since most catalogues are designed by computer programmers, with little input from library professionals or users.

Based on previous studies which investigated features that facilitate user performance, Shires and Olszak developed guidelines on how to design an effective OPAC screen with respect to the overall screen layout, menu screens, and enquiry screens. The authors included checklists in the article for designers to use. OPAC screen designers were reminded to create an interface that puts the users in control. Users should not feel helpless and lost when using OPACs. In order to ensure that user needs are dealt with during OPAC screen design, OPAC users, including librarians, should be informed of the latest developments in design and should be included in the design process.

For screen appearance, researchers recommended that information presented on the screen should have blank lines between different sets of information in order to improve user speed and accuracy in browsing the screen. Based on Galitz's book on computer interface screen design, Shires and Olszak concluded that an ideal screen should be orderly, clean, clutter-free, and the text on the screen should be balanced, symmetric, and in sequential order. They provided the following suggestions to interface designers and librarians:

- Maintain a user orientation
- Involve actual users in all phases of screen design: establishing, testing, and evaluating
- Formalise the involvement of actual users
- Establish a team or use other formal organisations to conduct the screen design process

Researchers encouraged librarians to inform patrons about the development of the interface and to include them in the process as active participants. Instead of reacting to products or being tested for performance, patrons should have some input before prototypes are constructed. Yee reviewed a number of user studies that examined various OPAC features including vocabulary, arrangement of multiple entries, and display of a single record. After she identified the problems with the existing designs.

The studies she reviewed revealed that users encountered the following problems: unclear abbreviations and initials, difficulty in understanding codes, and ambiguous brief displays. She concluded that in order to improve the effectiveness of a bibliographic display, more research is required to study the vocabulary for the bibliographic labels. When librarians have to choose an OPAC to purchase, the information available about the systems is usually technical. Little attention has been paid to the appropriateness of the systems from the users' point of view.

The design of an OPAC system should not be purely a computer programming enterprise. Crawford also reminded designers of OPAC user interfaces to understand their users' opinions. In other words, not only should the speed and accuracy of the users in locating information on a bibliographic display be taken into account when designing a new system, but users' opinions are worthy of researchers' and designers' attention.

BIBLIOGRAPHIC CONTENT

The main purpose for using a library catalogue is to search for desired materials. Library clients determine whether they have found what they were looking for based on the information presented on the bibliographic display. According to the *AACR2*, bibliographic information, from title to physical description, is used in a library catalogue to identify an item. However, library catalogue designers do not usually include all of the bibliographic information in the catalogue record on the screen.

In order to ensure that library clients are provided with the information they need, the design of bibliographic displays should take into account users' preferences in using this information. Before computerised library catalogues, bibliographic information was printed on 3×5-inch cards which together comprised the whole catalogue. Arguments about the necessary elements and the presentation of bibliographic information on OPAC displays have questioned whether the card tradition should be kept or changed. If changes are to be made, the next question is what they should be. In the early stage of OPAC development, researchers recommended the use of the conventional catalogue card format because users were familiar with it. Compared to a display with labels for the bibliographic elements, card or citation format consumes less space.

In spite of the familiarity and lower space consumption of the card format, the card-like presentation of bibliographic information has been generally rejected because computerised catalogues are regarded as fundamentally different from card catalogues with respect to capability and manipulability. The ease of modifying computerised catalogues provides library and information professionals with a chance to reform the old way of presenting bibliographic information. The large storage capability of computerised catalogues lets OPAC designers include information that could not have been available to users on 3×5-inch cards. Researchers reminded designers that, while they have new ideas for displaying bibliographic information, the positive characteristics of the old card system should not be completely ignored. Researchers devoted an entire book to discuss the issues related to designing effective bibliographic displays. The basis of this book was the testing of RLIN (Research Libraries Information Network) MARC (Machine-Readable Cataloguing) records.

The authors pointed out that different libraries have different needs, and researchers should not hope to create a single display to accommodate all libraries. Decisions on bibliographic display design should be based on the needs of local users and the nature of the library collection. However, in general, a display designer should pay attention to the following: fields and subfields; field grouping and arrangement; labelled or cardlike displays; what the labels are and where they should be; typography; display modes; and additional information. A successful bibliographic display should demonstrate the following characteristics:

- The display should provide an appropriate amount of information;
- Library users should understand the displayed information;
- The display should be readable and attractive;
- Library users should be able to locate necessary information on the screen rapidly; and
- All information should be displayed in a single screen.

Unlike card catalogues, OPACs usually present users with the option to obtain brief or long bibliographic displays. Brief displays should provide users with sufficient information to identify an item. The elements in a brief display should include: main entry; title statement; publisher; date of publication; and physical description. A long or full display should give users as much information as they would find useful. A survey of academic library users conducted by researchers showed that a bibliographic display with the following information should provide enough bibliographic information for the majority of users: Names; Title, Subtitle; Uniform Title; Subject Headings; Added Entries; Volume Number; Volume Title; Edition Statement; Date of Publication; Edition and History Note; References; ISBN or Control Number.

Additional information such as the location of the item, call number, circulation status, and presence of holds/reserves may also be included in a long bibliographic display. Researchers pointed out that OPACs should not be forced to inherit the old problems and misunderstandings of the traditional card system. The display of holdings, locations, and circulation status can help users reduce the amount of screen scanning and get all the desired information from a minimal number of screens.

These researchers constructed an evaluation checklist to examine various aspects of the OPAC systems. The researchers assessed the systems with respect to database characteristics, operational control, subject search code, output control, user assistance, and usability via remote access. In the database characteristics checklist, the researchers included sixteen items to evaluate how much information the OPACs provided to users. These sixteen items were:

1. Call number;
2. Author;
3. Title;
4. Subject heading(s);
5. Edition information;
6. Publication information;
7. Copy information;
8. Volume information;
9. Location for current issues of serials;
10. Name of the library where the item is located;
11. Loan status;
12. Document abstract;
13. Table of contents;
14. Citations within the text;
15. Keywords from the book index; and
16. Book review.

Although all the libraries received scores between 9 and 11, points were derived solely from items 1 to 11. None of the twelve libraries displayed information described in items 12 to 16 which previous researchers had suggested should be included in a bibliographic display.

BIBLIOGRAPHIC DISPLAY FORMAT

Once the list of elements to be displayed has been decided, designers have to consider various ways to arrange the elements on a screen. Although a screen is much larger than a

3×5-inch card, researcher pointed out that reading from the screen is more difficult than reading print material. To counter the problem, designers must be more liberal with the use of space in a display.

Further, space on a computer screen is less expensive than that on print material. Despite the necessity of including plenty of white/black space in an OPAC bibliographic display, researchers warned designers not to overuse spacing to improve screen appearance. Excessive use of space in bibliographic displays forces users to view the information on more than the necessary number of screens. In this case, designers face the risk that the users will view only the first screen and ignore the rest.

These principles refer to the text on the screen, screen density, and readability. In order to make the text displayed on the screen legible, the font used should be large and clear enough to make the information displayed stand out from the screen background. The content of the screen should not take up every space available. Researcher suggested that for bibliographic displays in a 25-line by 80-character screen, only 30 per cent of the screen should be used for content. Thirty percent of the screen translates to 600 characters or about 100 words. Readability can be improved by observing the following guidelines.

The text in each line should occupy no more than 60 to 65 characters. Enough space should be provided for labels to be spelled out. Blank lines and other white space should be used intelligently to enhance readability. However, the use of double spacing would lead to the loss of coherence in the text. Printing in all uppercase makes scanning difficult. Instead of using all capital letters, designers should effectively employ other different types of highlighting techniques like bold, italic, colours, and reverse video. However, researcher advised designers not to use more than two or three different techniques in a single screen. Designers should also keep in mind that the same highlighting technique should not be applied to different purposes.

For example, if the labels are in bold, instructions should not be in bold as well. In addition to the bibliographic displays should only display information that users require and the information should be placed in a sequence users would expect. Researchers investigated how a labelled format differed from the standard Library of Congress (LC) or card format in terms of time required for users to locate specific bibliographic information and in terms of users' preferences. Using the data collected from 340 university students.

In addition, users indicated preferences for displays with labels over the traditional card format. Researchers attributed this preference to the fact that the labelled display was easily understood and required little effort to scan by the users. Hence, labels deserve special attention in their design and vocabulary. Researcher discussed format guidelines specifically for label and asserted that labels should be:

- In uppercase;
- Spelled out as words, not abbreviations;
- Used for all fields;
- Right-justified;
- Separated from the text using a colon (:) and at least one blank space;
- Between 12 and 20 characters long; and
- Displayed in columns.

The objective of designing labels with the guidelines is to ensure that the labels are distinguishable from the text. The choice of terms used in labels is as complex as the format used to display them. The labels used in bibliographic displays tend to mean something different from the usual meanings of the terms. The label "TI" or "Title" is often more than simply the title of the item because users can find title statement, collation (physical description), and imprint (place, publisher, date of publication) under this label. Not only would users be confused by the labels, but the vocabulary used in labels varies from catalogue to catalogue.

Users can be easily confused by the type of information grouped together by a system but treated separately in another. Many guidelines exist for designing bibliographic displays, some based on user performance and some based on user preference. Researchers have noted that the many variations in elements and formats in bibliographic displays require research to search for a standard that will facilitate user performance and improve user satisfaction. Chan designed a checklist to evaluate OPAC bibliographic displays. The checklist consists of four sections to assess how well a bibliographic display follows the guidelines suggested by researchers: labels, text, instructional information, and screen layout. Researcher applied the checklist to twelve academic and ten public OPACs in Canada.

Her results demonstrated the wide gap between design guidelines and the existing displays. The average score for the academic libraries was 59 per cent with a range of 49 per cent to 70 per cent. On the other hand, the public libraries averaged 55 per cent with a range of 52 per cent to 59 per cent. Among the four areas the checklist addressed, screen layout appeared to be the primary cause for such low scores. This checklist provides an evaluation tool and can also serve as a guide for designing new displays.

THE TECHNIQUE OF FOCUS GROUPS

Focus groups, a qualitative research method, have often been used by marketing professionals to learn about customers' attitudes towards a product. Compared to other qualitative methods like field studies, focus groups offer a better approach for studying people's attitudes and thoughts because participants have opportunities to elaborate on their opinions. Results obtained through focus groups can be used as a self-contained study or part of a large project. Stewart and Shamdasani suggested that focus groups can be used for: obtaining general background information about a topic; creating hypotheses to be tested with quantitative methods; generating new ideas and concepts; evaluating a product, a service, or a programme; developing questionnaires or other research tools using the information obtained; and interpreting previous quantitative results.

The validity of focus groups, like other research methods, depends on the research questions and the context. Several authors provide guidelines for conducting effective focus groups. The guidelines address the characteristics of the participants based on the research topic, the number of sessions, the number of participants per session, and the moderator's level of involvement. Researcher suggested six to eight participants for unstructured focus groups and three to four for structured ones.

Generally, the recommended number of participants per session falls within the range of four to ten. Too few participants may limit the diversity of discussion, while too many may prove hard for the moderator to control. The source of participants is also addressed by the guidelines. Although the sample does not have to be representative of the population because generalisation is not the goal of focus groups, participants should present a wide range of opinions regarding the topic.

Depending on the topic of discussion, participants should be homogeneous in order to promote free discussion. For example, a discussion of health care policy should group participants by age because different age groups have different concerns regarding health care. In order to ensure that all opinions are exposed and discussed in depth, grouping by age is necessary. Finally, the moderator's level of involvement in the focus group sessions must be selected. This will influence how the groups perform.

A low level of involvement is important for exploratory type of research, whereas a high level of involvement is effective if the focus groups are conducted according to a clearly stated agenda. Compared to other qualitative research methods, focus groups are less expensive and more flexible because focus groups require fewer participants than surveys and less time than interviews.

THE USE OF FOCUS GROUPS IN LIBRARY AND INFORMATION SCIENCE

Researchers used focus groups to study user opinions about local library service. Baker used twelve questions to probe for opinions regarding Iowa City Public Library's special service for the business community. Participants recruited from the business community provided suggestions with respect to equipment and facilities to the library in order to assist the library to better serve the business community.

This focus group project served as an opportunity not only to collect opinions from clients, but also to spread the news of this special service to the community and to promote the library's public relations. Researchers used focus groups to investigate the attitudes of Purdue University students concerning the quality of the library service. Data collected from the focus groups supplemented the data obtained earlier in a questionnaire survey. Students expressed opinions pertaining to the library's long term planning such as catalogue system centralisation and to its current services including the availability of photocopiers. The researchers from both studies recommended the method of focus groups as a research tool in the field of library science. As part of the Council of Library Resources (CLR) nationwide study of OPACs and their use, Kaske used focus groups to validate and expand the data previously obtained from a questionnaire survey.

In the CLR study, researchers recruited 440 OPAC users and non-users from six different libraries. After interviewing 70 groups of library clients, the researchers discovered about 60 themes concerning OPACs. These themes were grouped into four categories: existing system(s); card to computer transition; database; and user assistance. After reviewing Kaske's study, Drabenstott concluded that focus groups are "an effective method for identifying people's feelings and beliefs about situations, products, and services and how these shape their behaviour."

The advantages of focus groups have not been fully exploited by the OPAC researchers. One could say that OPAC is a service that a library provides to its clients. Therefore, the opinions and comments of the clients regarding the OPAC system can be obtained through focus groups.

10

Staff Opinions in Library Automation Planning

For the library automation planner faced with the need to oversee the implementation of a system, however, there are few descriptions of how successful projects have developed or maintained effective communication with the library staff. The following is a description of one library's efforts to increase understanding of its automation needs and planning.

BACKGROUND

The Indiana State Library in Indianapolis employs approximately 80 people, of whom about 45 per cent are professional librarians. The library's seven divisions are housed in a three-story building in the center of Indianapolis. Connected to Indiana's State Capitol and State Office Building, the library provides information and services for state legislators and state employees, as well as offers a number of other specialised services, notably materials for the blind and physically handicapped, support for genealogical and historical research, and support for public libraries in the state. A fairly decentralised structure has developed as staff in various divisions have sought to provide excellent service to their respective clientele.

Since the 1970s, the library has used OCLC for much of its cataloging and interlibrary loans. The general card catalog was frozen in January 1981 when a COM catalog was produced to provide catalog access. A printed subject catalog for the genealogy collection was produced at the same time. These catalogs, generated from OCLC tapes, included items cataloged from the mid-1970s through the date of catalog production.

The listings were intended to be cumulated and reissued annually, with quarterly updates. A variety of technical and contractual problems disruvted this schedule-the nadir being a nine-month wait for any new catalog listing in 1982. The library has access to external automated systems for reference service. In addition, the library director uses his personal microcomputer for budget planning, and state-wide public library statistics have been prepared on the state's mainframe computer since 1980. However, there was no general access to computers or automation during the period described by this report, and circulation was handled manually by each division of the library.

Automated support was requested to deal with heavy and increasing circulation in materials for the blind and physically handicapped, as well as problems of delays in the library's COM catalog and lack of library-wide knowledge about special collections. The state government approved preparing a request for proposals for a turn-key on-line catalog and circulation system. However, all activity was stopped in 1981 due to a budget freeze. The resulting sense of frustration was compounded by low staff involvement in automation planning.

Staff morale was generally considered poor, and opinions about automation were presumed to be negative. At the same time, it was necessary to involve the library staff both in selecting an automated system which would do the best possible job of meeting the wide variety of needs in the library and in encouraging staff acceptance of the system. With these goals in mind, four librarians worked with a consultant from the Indiana University School of Library and Information Science to develop a survey of staff opinion regarding automation.

It was hoped that soliciting staff opinions would help suggest areas of staff concern to be addressed in planning for automation and provide a benchmark with which to compare changes in attitudes during the automation process. A survey of all staff was conducted in 1983 and repeated a year later.

FIRST STAFF OPINION QUESTIONNAIRE

The questionnaire primarily focused on attitudes towards automation and expectations of the library automation project. Impressions of staffing and training implications of the library automation plans were solicited, as well as "reactions to automation." Some background on respondents' division of work and experience with computers was collected in case it became necessary to target specific audiences, and people were asked to indicate which means of providing information on automation plans were desirable. An open-ended request for comments or observations concluded the survey form, which is reproduced, with the number of responses to each question. The questionnaire was distributed in April 1983, with a cover letter from the library director.

Response was voluntary, and work time could be used to complete the questionnaires, which were returned anonymously. Fifty-nine responses were received from 77 employees-a response rate of approximately 77 per cent. Respondents indicated they would like to be involved in planning for an automated system through discussion sessions, serving on automation committees, and reviewing and commenting on automation priorities. There was significant interest in being kept informed on automation efforts, with training sessions, general meetings, circulation of automation plans, tours of other libraries, and vendor demonstrations receiving high ratings.

AUTOMATION PLANNING AND STAFF INVOLVEMENT

The survey results were summarised at two open meetings for all library staff. Here the library director asked for volunteers to serve on two new, librarywide committees: a library automation planning committee and a staff development committee. The director appointed all senior administrators to the library automation planning committee, and 14 other employees volunteered to serve on the committee. The committee organised subcomittees to investigate word processing options, and to review and update the statement of the library's requirements of an on-line catalog and circulation system. These groups provided opportunities to learn about the complexity of automation needs and the relatively strict monetary constraints that determined what the library could afford.

In addition, subcommittee members shared their tasks with staff from other divisions of the library, reducing some of the parochial attitudes which result from the decentralised organisation. Eventually word processing recommendations were forwarded to the library director. Shortly thereafter the request for proposals was revised, approved through the state's review process, and released. The eight-member, staff development committee concentrated initially on staff development for automation. The committee published an almost-monthly news memo to continue dissemination of automation plans begun at the open meetings. A question box was designed, and its contributions provided topics for the news memo.

In addition, several programmes were organised to acquaint staff with automation terminology, to visit the local public library's automated system, and to conduct demonstrations of microcomputers owned by staff members. One especially effective programme involved a discussion by public librarians of their experiences during the installation of an on-line catalog and circulation system. This process provided increasing staff awareness of the library's automation plans, particularly relating to word processing and the on-line catalog and circulation system. However, there was little tangible evidence of increasing automation. A terminal to reach the state's mainframe computer was installed in the library building, but no other computer equipment appeared.

SECOND STAFF OPINION QUESTIONNAIRE

In April 1984, one year after the first survey, a second testing of staff opinion was done. This questionnaire repeated many items from the first one, while incorporating some changes to reflect the then current situations with word processing and on-line catalog planning. There was relatively little turnover in staff, and four positions had been filled in the intervening year, leaving the surveyed population fairly stable. Fiftyseven responses were received from 81 employees-a response rate of 70 per cent. The survey form, with the number of responses to each question, is reproduced.

COMPARISON OF SURVEY RESPONSES

In comparing responses for the two surveys, statistically significant changes occurred in respondents' perceptions of having been kept informed about automation efforts.

Table 10.1 Staff Perceptions of Being Informed about Automation Plans

Do you feel you have been kept informed on the Library's automation plans?

	-1983	-1984
yes	26	53
no	26	0
don't know	6	3
chi square = 36.073,		
degrees of freedom	=	2. *0* <.001

Ninety-five per cent of respondents to the second survey reported that they had been kept informed, compared with only 45 per cent a year earlier. Several of the open-ended comments praised the staff development committee's work in this area. An equally significant change appeared in perceptions of how staff attitudes were affected by automation.

Table 10.2 Effects of Automation on Staff Attitudes

How have library automation efforts to date affected staff attitudes?

	-1983	-1984
attitudes have improved automation efforts have had no	10	21
impact on staff attitudes	14	15
attitudes have deteriorated	16	2
don't know	19	17
chi square = 14.8 16, degrees of freedom =	3, p <.01	

As the comparison in table shows, 27 per cent of year one respondents felt automation had caused attitudes to deteriorate. One year later this had fallen to 4 per cent. The list of possible reactions to automation was divided into two categories: positive and negative. The negative reactions were further divided into groups roughly based on three of Kotter and Schlesinger's four most common reasons people resist change: different assessment of library's needs, low tolerance for change, and parochial self interest. These categories and the number of responses to each are given in table.

Table 10.3 Staff Reactions to Automation at the Library

	1983	{N = 77}	1984	{N = 57}
Positive reactions to automation	176	(85.4%)	180	(87.8%)
Improve services	48	(23.3%)	47	(22.9%)
Good idea	38	(18.4%)	42	(20.0%)
Improve prestige	24	(11.6%)	24	(11.7%)
Work will be more Interesting	22	(10.7%)	24	(11.7%)
Would help my Carrer	22	(10.7%)	19	(9.2%)
It's about time	22	(10.7%)	24	(11.7%)
Negative reactions to automation	30	(14.6%)	25	(12.2%)
Different Assessment of Needs money Better spent on Other services	11	(5.3%)	4	(1.9%)
Costs too much	7	(3.4%)	7	(3.4%)
Not needed	1	(0.5%)	7	(0.5%)
Low tolerance for Change Apprehensive	10	(4.9%)	8	(3.9%)
I would quit if the library automated	0	(0%)	0	(0%)
Parochial Seif Interest work Would be More Boring	0	(0%)	1	(0.5%)
Who cares	0	(0%)	2	(1.0%)
Too much work	1	(0.5%)	2	(1.0%)
Total	**206**	**(100%)**	**205**	**(100%)**

Although negative opinions had been expected, especially in the first survey, the vast majority of the responses (over 85 per cent) was positive. The negative reactions were due mainly to a different assessment of the library's needs or a low tolerance for change. However, the only low tolerance for change reaction selected was "apprehensive," much less negative than the "I would quit if the library automated" reaction, which was not chosen by any of the respondents.

The second year's responses were slightly more positive, but the frequency ranking of each reaction remained remarkably stable. Reactions chosen most often were that automation would improve services and that it was "a good idea." The other positive reactions each accounted for about 10 per cent of the responses. The major change from the first to the second survey was a decline in the proportion of respondents who felt that the money would be better spent on other services (down from 5.3 per cent to 1.9 per cent). Expectations of how automation would affect jobs underwent some changes.

In the first survey 42 per cent of respondents thought staff would be transferred or laid off, while 34 per cent did not know what implication automation held for staffing. One year later only 25 per cent expected transfers or layoffs, but 73 per cent were uncertain of staffing implications. This change was significant -probably reflecting the general improvement in State financial conditions, as well as uncertainty about the proposed automation project. A comparison of response rates to several of these questions is presented in table.

Table 10.4 Expectations of Impact of On-line Catalog and Circulation

	1983	{N = 77}	1984	{N = 57}
Library services will be improved	44	(36%)	43	(39%)
Faster	44	(36%)	35	(32%)
Less personal	9	(7%)	11	(10%)
More complicated	12	(10%)	5	(5%)
About the same	5	(4%)	7	(6%)
Don't know	5	(4%)	4	(4%)
Deteriorated	0	(0%)	4	(4%)
Slower	3	(3%)	0	(0%)
Change in your job will be major	16	(27%)	9	(16%)
Minor or none	25	(42%)	38	(68%)
Retraining will e required for my position	19	(32%)	13	(23%)
Your job classification will be upgraded	4	(6%)	1	(2%)
Downgraded	1	(2%)	0	(0%)
Work will be about the same	16	(21%)	34	(48%)
More fun	21	(28%)	13	(18%)
Less complicated	12	(16%)	9	(13%)
More complicated	14	(19%)	5	(7%)
Less personal	2	(3%)	3	(4%)
Don't know	10	(13%)	7	(10%)
My work load will increase	12	(21%)	10	(18%)
Decrease	3	(5%)	3	(5%0

Major changes in jobs were expected by 27 per cent in the first year, with 32 per cent expecting retraining. By the second year only 16 per cent expected major changes, and 23 per cent foresaw retraining ($p < .05$). Anticipated changes in job classifications or workload were not significant.

The percentage of respondents expecting job upgrades declined by the second year, while no one anticipated downgrading. Expectations of workload changes remained stable, with close to 20 per cent expecting an increase and about 5 per cent a decrease in workload. Changes also occurred in perceptions of work with an automated system. The percentage who expected work to be "about the same" increased, while those anticipating work to be either "more fun" or "more complicated declined. Perceptions of automation's impact on library services did not change significantly.

Most people felt services would be improved and faster, though the next two most frequent choices were "less personal" and "more complicated." A major shift occurred in the latter, with a drop from 10 per cent to 5 per cent of respondents expecting services to be more complicated. The idea that an automated system may not be as complicated as first thought parallels the assessment work may not be as complicated either. A remarkable difference between the two surveys was the number of responses to the open-ended request to "share any comments or observations you have on automation at the State Library."

Thirtyeight people (64 per cent) commented on the first survey, often in carefully thoughtout essays of two or three paragraphs, bringing out a variety of concerns. Only 26 people (46 per cent) responded to the request for comments a year later, and 19 of the comments (73 per cent) were primarily in response to the request for suggestions on staff development needs. A summary of the comments is given in table.

Even with the decline in the number of people making general comments, the percentage of comments in most sections remained about the same. The major shift was from a focus on past problems at the library to expanding on the observation that staff are better informed.

Table 10.5 Summary of Staff Comments

	1983		1984	
Staff fears and need for training	15	(27%)	7	(28%)
Concern about specific library services	12	(21%)	4	(16%)
Past problems with automation at library	12	(21%)	0	(0%)
Questions of funding support or priorities	10	(18%)	6	(24%)
General positive comments	7	(13%)	3	(12%)
Staff are better informed	0	(0%)	5	(20%)
Total	**56**	**(100%)**	**25**	**(100%)**

CONCLUSION

Responses to the two surveys of Indiana State Library staff indicate major changes in sense of involvement and assessment of automation's impact on staff attitudes. At the same time, reactions to automation in general remained quite positive and relatively stable. By the second year fewer people expected that work with an on-line catalog and circulation system would be greatly different from existing operations. Several changes occurred at the library during the year between the surveys, but respondents' comments indicate that the use of library automation planning and staff development committees were in part responsible for the changes observed.

The use of written news memos, general meetings, and specialised subcommittees provided opportunities for staff to both expand their knowledge and contribute to the automation process.

11

Evaluation of Electronic Reference Sources

INTRODUCTION

Today information technology (IT) has been playing an important role for every section of the society. Its impact is visible in almost all walks of life and libraries are no exception to it. Since the users today have multi-dimensional requirements, IT is gaining fast access in libraries, information centres and documentation centres to meet their changing requirements and provide value-added and need-based services to its users. It has affected not only the way of acquiring and processing the documents/information in the libraries but also the way of providing the reference service to the users of the library.

The field of reference service is very vast and dynamic. The basic purpose of any library however small or big it may be, remains the same, *i.e.*, to collect, organise and disseminate the information to meet the information requirements of its users. Technological development particularly with the introduction of computer technology, communication technology, printing technology, reprography, etc., have added new dimensions to the role of librarians in the dissemination of information.

With the introduction of IT, advances have been made not only in the format of reference sources but also in the manner of providing reference service. One can have direct access to computerised databases via terminals or the needed information can be made available to the client through internet in no time, irrespective of where the information is available. Today the emphasis in the libraries is shifting from 'acquisition of documents' to 'access to information' thereby increasing the scope of reference service to 'no limit extent'. Libraries are passing through a revolutionary phase which has changed the way of working of professionals in the libraries. Under the changing scenario, library professionals are expected to be well acquainted with all these developments which would help to meet the challenges of today.

One should know how to use computer for providing reference service, what the various forms available of electronic reference sources are, how to access them, and how to select the best of these sources. Today any reference librarian can provide a wealth of information by acquiring non-print form of documents such as CD-ROMs and online databases. Unlike print documents, for accessing the electronic documents one has to rely upon the equipment required to access such documents.

Till recently paper form of reference sources was the only form available in the libraries for the users. The students in library science schools in India were taught how to evaluate the print form of reference sources to enable them to acquire the best reference sources in their library. But since most of the libraries today are going for computerisation and are acquiring reference sources in CD-ROMs and online forms, it has become necessary to have a knowledge regarding how to evaluate CD-ROMs and online reference sources for their acquisition in the libraries.

CHARACTERISTICS OF REFERENCE SOURCES

- These form a special category of documents meant for consultation or reference and not for consecutive reading.
- These are secondary or tertiary sources based on primary or secondary sources of information.
- Usually these are compiled works for which information is gathered from a large number of

sources. These sources do not contain new knowledge, but contain the knowledge which is already available somewhere.

- In such sources information is organised according to some definite artificial plan of arrangement which can provide fast access to information in the most convenient manner.
- These sources have disjointed entries, having no line by line or para by para relationship as is there in other sources. So they have no continuity of thought contents as a result, these cannot be read para by para or page by page.
- Such sources are comprehensive in coverage (scope) and condensed in treatment.
- These are not 100 per cent reliable for the data or information provided therein.

EVALUATION

Evaluation of reference sources in a library context means assessing the value of the source according to the requirements of the library, based on users' level of education. For any library, the process of evaluation is very important to develop the need-based best collection. It helps to assess the value or evaluate the quality of a particular source and also it's suitability for inclusion in the library collection depending upon the readership of the library. Various approaches have been suggested by different authorities like Katz, Smith, and Gates, etc. Although originally the evaluation criteria were developed for printed sources, but they can equally be used for evaluation of electronic sources (e-sources). However, in case of e-sources some additional points are also needed.

CRITERIA FOR EVALUATION

With the tremendous inflow of information being generated from vast range of sources, it has become essential to evaluate the information for conducting quality research. For this purpose, each source of information must be reviewed with due care to ensure the authority, accuracy, quality, reliability and objectivity of the information one uses. This section describes the general criteria which may be used for evaluation of electronic (internet) reference sources.

Purpose

The first thing is to find out the purpose of publishing the source? Is it to inform, to sell or to entertain? Web sites can be misleading in their stated or implied purpose. Therefore, purpose of site should be carefully seen.

Authority

It is necessary to find who is the author, is he/she a known expert/scholar? What is the author's occupation, position, title, education, experience, etc.? Is the page signed? Is the author qualified to write on the subject? What were the sources (primary or secondary) of author's information/knowledge? Are these sources cited as bibliography? Has he explored new sources, and were they well chosen and sufficient for the purpose? In case of web sources, it may be difficult to determine authors and their qualifications (even if the page is signed) as any one can publish anything on web, moreover, these are not regulated for quality and accuracy as a result, user has to be more alert to know whether the information can be verified? Is the information filtered, *i.e.*, peer-reviewed? Has it been refereed? One should check URL domain for source of information and find who the publisher of document is and what are its credentials. Is the publisher well known with good experience and reputation for issuing reference sources. Is he a recognised authority? Availability of e-mail address, phone number of authors/publishers can help in authentication of information and sources.

Accuracy

Accuracy is a very important characteristic for any source so one should assess if the information is accurate? Can it be checked for its accuracy? Is there an editor or someone who verifies/checks the information? How does it compare with other sources of information? Are the sources for factual information clearly listed for verification of information? Is it clear who has the ultimate responsibility for accuracy of information? Has the information been reviewed or refereed? Is it free from grammatical, spellings, or typographical errors?

Objectivity

A standard source is the one which reflects clear objectivity of information, therefore one should check is the information biased? Does it project all perspectives on an issue? Is the author's point of view objective and impartial? Does it reflect the author's (bias) affiliation with an organisation? Whether the information provided is a fact, opinion, or propaganda? Is the information free of advertising? Does the content of the page has an official approval of the institution? One should also find when the information was published and is the information in its original form or has been revised?

Currency

Although the currency of information usually depends upon the nature of the topic. It is particularly important in science and technology where information changes very fast. However, a good reference source should be updated regularly, therefore, one should always try to find when the information was first published? When it was updated and is it recent enough for the needed purpose? Is the site updated regularly? Is there any indication when the site was last updated? Dates are sometimes absent or may have different meanings like date of creation, placing on web or last revised, so one should check the dates carefully.

Reliability

It is important to check the reliability and credibility of sources. Is it authentic? One should ascertain why to believe information given on the site? Does the information appear to be valid and well researched or it is unsupported by evidence? Is the information unique or has it been copied? Which institution supports this information? Is the supporting institution well known? Are there some non-web equivalents of the material to verify the information?

Coverage

Is the source comprehensive enough in its coverage for the indicated needs of the audience? What items are included? What subject area, time period, formats, or type of materials are covered in the site? Does the site contain original information or simply links? If links are given, what kind of sources are linked, are these related to the topic and useful for the purpose of the site? Are these links still current or they have become dead ends? Have these been evaluated or annotated in any way?

Format and Presentation

Is the information easy to get? Does the source contain a table of contents and/or an index to facilitate the use or to find the specific information one needs? How many links does it take to provide the needed information? Is the arrangement of links uncluttered? Does the site has its own search engine? Is the site easily browsable and searchable? If graphical images are included, what is the quality of these graphical images? Do these images enhance the understanding of the resource or distract from the content?

Special Features

Does the source contain graphs, charts, tables, maps, or any other special features that adds to the usefulness of the source? Does it use header and footer to indicate information about the author and source?

EXAMPLES OF E-SOURCES

Now a good number of reference sources are available on internet and CD-ROMs.

ON INTERNET

- Encyclopaedia Britannica Online
- http://www.eb.com

- http://www.britannica
- Rogets International Thesaurus Online
- http://www.thesaurus.com
- http://www.encyclopaedia.com
- Webster's Dictionary
- http://www.dictionary.com
- http://www.m-w.com
- Encyclopaedias and Almanacs
- http://www.virtualref.com/libdocs/
- Newspapers Directory
- http://www.newsrack.com
- http://www.samachar.com

IN CD-ROM FORMAT

CD-ROM is another pub lish ing me dium fall ing un der the eco nomic cat e gory of elec tronic sources avail able in most of the Indian li braries. It is ca pable of con taining enor mous quan tity of in for ma tion. Most of the Indian li brar ies are us ing this me dium these days to ful fil their us ers' re quirements in an eco nomic way. This form has been found to be eco nomic, par ticularly when one and the same source is to be used by many us ers again and again.

CONCLUSION

For evaluating web documents, author or contact person with address (e-mail); document URL, including an institution identifier (*e.g.*, edu); date of creation or revision and link to sponsoring institution web site may be used. For evaluating esources one should be very critical of any information found on web, and it should be carefully examined. Information available on the internet is not regulated for quality and accuracy, therefore it is particularly important to evaluate the internet resources or information. Since anyone can publish anything on web and it is often difficult to determine authorship of web sources, therefore, the responsibility of the librarian increases manifolds to evaluate such resources still more carefully. Web pages are susceptible to both accidental and deliberate alterations and may disappear without any notice. Other sources like print may also be used as they may be sometimes more comprehensive in nature. As there are few quality controls on the internet, one must use the same guidelines as for printed sources but apply these guidelines even more rigourously. Most important thing about internet sources is to know links given to other web pages are current as well as the qualitative in nature.

Bibliography

Augustine: *Developing Multi-media Libraries*, Boston: William J. Nagel Company, 2001.

Baruah, S.: *The Library and Information Sector: Core Knowledge, Skills and Attributes*, New Delhi: Oxford University Press, 2003.

Berners-Lee, T.: *Developing Libraries Cataloguing*, San Francisco: Harper Bowling Green State University, 2000.

Bonura, Larry S.: *The Art of Indexing*, New York: John Wiley & Sons, 1994.

Borko, Horald, and Bernier, Charles L.: *Abstracting Concepts and Methods*, New York: Academic Press, 1975.

Borko, Horald, and Bernier, Charles L.: *Indexing Concepts and Methods*, New York: Academic Press, 1978.

Mercado, H.: *Library Automation*, Brisbane: Australian Academic Press, 2003.

Moshinskie, J.: *How Libraries Collect and Handle Artists' Books*, UK: Univesity of Minnesota, 2000.

Coulthard: *Characteristics and Experiences of Integrated Library Systems Installations*, London: Longman Press, 2005.

Gururaj, G.: *Library Classification: Evolution of a Dynamic Theory*, Dharwar: Karnataka University Press, 2007.

Khan, B.H.: *Selection and Acquisition in an Art School Library*, India: Educational Technology Publications, 2001.

Lynch, M. J.: *Reference Interviews in Public Libraries*, New York: Cambridge University Press, 2003.

Newton, R.: *Staff Attitudes to the Development in Library*, India: Cambridge University Press, 2005.

Pursell, G.: *Preservation Microfilming: A Guide for Librarians and Archivists*, London: Sage Publications, 2002.

Raye, R.: *Subject Searching Behaviour at the Library Catalogue and at the Shelves: Implications for Online Interactive Catalogues*, New York: American Geographical Society, 2002.

Reynolds, Paul D.: *Video Preservation Handbook*, Kansas City: Kauffman Center, 2005.

Sen, A.: *Encyclopedia of Library and Information Science*, Delhi: Oxford University Press, 2002.

Sharma S.C.: *Building Embedded Linux Systems*, Kolkata: Magnum Press, 2000.

Singh A. Lalit: *Staffing the Modern Library*, Mumbai: Mittal Publications, 2004.

Tirmare, P.: *Library Cataloging: Issues and Facts*, Maharashtra: Pune University, 2000.

Webstar, J.: *Library Cataloging in Modern Indian Libraries*, New Delhi: Vistar Publications, 2001.

Zelliot, E.: *Dr. Wynar's Introduction to Cataloging and Classification*, New Delhi: Jain Publications, 2003.

Index

L

M

O

P

R

S

T

U